I Love To Write Day

Creative Writing Journal

John Riddle

Celebrate I Love To Write Day
On November 15th

Welcome to the I Love To Write Day

Creative Writing Journal

First of all, THANK YOU for buying this journal! Your support of I Love To Write Day is very much appreciated.

Special thanks go out to three authors and their books who not only gave me the inspiration for this journal, but they also provided the "hey, do it now!" motivation I needed to get it done.

1. Sam Horn, Founder and CEO of the Intrigue Agency, is a communications strategist and international consultant. She has been featured on just about every media outlet on the planet, AND she has written many books. One that I HIGHLY RECOMMEND is *Someday Is Not a Day in the Week.*

2. Samuel Sanders is an award-winning entrepreneur who has seen entrepreneurship, innovation, creativity, problem-solving and ideation in action at many companies (including ones he launched himself). His book, *Your Next Big Idea: Improve Your Creativity and Problem Solving,* is also HIGHLY RECOMMENDED.

3. Michael F. Schein is the Founder and President of Microfame Media, a marketing agency that specializes in turning consultants, entrepreneurs, and executives into celebrities by using the hype concepts in his book, *The Hype Handbook: 12 Indispensable Success Secrets From the World's Greatest Propagandists, Self-Promoters, Cult Leaders, Mischief Makers, and Boundary Breakers.* His book needs to be on your MUST READ list.

I launched I Love To Write Day in 2002 as a grassroots campaign to have people of all ages spend time writing every November 15th.

Over the past two decades there have been many success stories. Schools, colleges, writing groups, writers, authors, editors, artists, bookstores and even a few malls have joined in the fun by celebrating I Love To Write Day.

Learn more about I Love To Write Day at

ilovetowriteday.com

The journal is filled with lots of blank pages, so you and "create and go wild" as your imagination leads you. There are also 30 "creative challenges" for you to enjoy.

You'll also find lots of "creative tips" and "how I am creative" ideas from over 80 creative people all around the globe.

Ready...Set...Create!

Creative Challenges...

A quick note before you begin these fun creative challenges...

In some cases, there will be enough lines or blank pages for you to complete the challenges. In other cases, it will be easier to write on a tablet (not the electronic kind!), a typewriter (hey, some people still use them!) or your computer or smartphone.

I must confess, that in my early years of attending Catholic school, the nuns pretty much told us we would "burn in hell" if we wrote in any of the textbooks, LOL.

So, it took me many years before I was brave enough to actually write in a journal that I purchased. Hopefully, you won't have that problem!

CREATIVE CHALLENGES...

Creative Challenge #1

Create your own special day!

I launched I Love To Write Day in 2002 as a grassroots campaign to have people of all ages spend time writing every Nov. 15th. I was on my way to teach a few writing workshops at the Blue Ridge Mountain Christian Writer's Conference in Ashville, North Carolina, when I stopped at a diner and got the idea. Somewhere in my collection of writing memorabilia I still have the napkin where I wrote the words "I Love To Write Day!"

After the conference I started sending out e-mails, press releases, articles and info about I Love To Write Day to media outlets, writing groups, journalists, schools and just about anyone else I could think of.

USA Today interviewed me and ran a story about ILTWD on the first Nov. 15th celebration, which helped give us the boost we needed.

So, what special day can you create? Search online and you will literally find a "special day" on every day of the week. But don't let that stop you...I share I Love To Write Day with "National Clean Out Your Refrigerator Day!"

Ready...Set...Create!

_____

_____

_____

_____

_____

Creative Challenge #2

Your creative challenge is to make a list of how you will deal with a project, when you are "stuck" and feel like you can't go on.

For example, when I'm stuck, I do any number of the following things:

- Take a break and watch a funny movie.
- Go to the mall.
- Eat some ice cream.
- Go for a walk.

Now it's your turn...make a list (and make sure it includes lots of fun things to do!).

Ready...Set...Create!

Creative Challenge #3

Your creative challenge is to make a list of people and places you want to contact!

When is the last time you wrote a letter...or an e-mail to someone or someplace just to say "hi" or "thanks?"

My obsession with writing began when I was in grade school. I wrote to the Director of the FBI (after watching a boatload of the "The FBI" TV series with Efrem Zimbalist Jr.) A few weeks later I received a package from the FBI, containing a letter, thanking me for writing to them, and a whole bunch of stuff that every boy my age would enjoy: Wanted Posters, A Fingerprint Kit and more!

Next, I wrote to the Commandant of the Coast Guard, asking about Lighthouses, and also received a nice letter and lots of info.

A few years ago, I wrote to about a dozen authors, both famous and not so famous ones, and received snail mail replies from 10 of them. A few were "form letters," thanking me for my interest, etc., but many were handwritten and personal.

So, put on your brainstorming hat and come up with a list of 6 people or places you will contact (bonus points if you reach out via snail mail!):

1.＿＿＿＿＿＿＿＿＿＿＿＿＿＿＿＿＿＿＿

2.＿＿＿＿＿＿＿＿＿＿＿＿＿＿＿＿＿＿＿

3.＿＿＿＿＿＿＿＿＿＿＿＿＿＿＿＿＿＿＿

4.＿＿＿＿＿＿＿＿＿＿＿＿＿＿＿＿＿＿＿

5.＿＿＿＿＿＿＿＿＿＿＿＿＿＿＿＿＿＿＿

6.＿＿＿＿＿＿＿＿＿＿＿＿＿＿＿＿＿＿＿

Make sure you follow through and write to them!

Creative Challenge #4

Your creative challenge is to come up with a new Christmas holiday special!

Here are the top 5 reasons why I have always loved Christmas:

1. It's the best "feel good" season!
2. The decorations, lights and other holiday scenes are the best!
3. Presents, presents and more presents! (Spoiler alert: as I got older, I realized I enjoyed GIVING presents more than I did RECEIVING them!)
4. This one is a tie between going to see Christmas shows and events in person, and performing in Christmas shows! One time I saw the "Rockettes" at Radio City Music Hall in New York City! And I was in 5 different Christmas plays at the Everett Theater in Middletown, Delaware.
5. The Christmas Specials on television.

One of my all-time favorite Christmas specials on television is "A Charlie Brown Christmas." Way back in 1965 it was shown on TV for the first time, and it was a big hit! There were no DVD's, VCR's or streaming services in those days, which meant that if you didn't watch "A Charlie Brown Christmas" when it was on TV, you had to wait an entire year before you could catch it again!

What is your all-time favorite Christmas special?

In the meantime, put on your brainstorming hat, and create a Christmas holiday special that everyone will enjoy watching!

Ready...Set...Create!

_____

_____

_____

_____

_____

_____

_____

_____

Creative Challenge #5

Create a new cartoon character!

When I was growing up, there were only 3 TV channels. When I was about 12 years old, I think they added a few more.

Every Saturday morning you could count on watching some of your favorite cartoons on TV. Almost everyone I knew would grab a bowl of cereal, and sit in the living room on the floor...watching cartoons!

I remember watching lots of different cartoons, including "The Flintstones," "Yogi Bear," "Huckleberry Hound," "Tom and Jerry," and one of my all-time favorites: "Mighty Mouse."

"Mighty Mouse" was originally created to be a "fly" instead of a mouse. Somehow, I cannot imagine a "fly" flying around wearing a cape; but for some reason, a "flying mouse with super powers" was more fun to watch!

Each week "Mighty Mouse" would have an adventure where he would save the day and defeat the bad guys.

So, put on your brainstorming hat and create a new cartoon character! AND, come up with a few story lines for that character.

BE BRAVE!

Creative Challenge #6

When were you scared reading a book or watching a movie?

I served on 3 Destroyers as a Quartermaster from 1970 to 1974. My job as a navigator kept me on the bridge, and there were times when the seas were so rough, waves were crashing 10 to 20 feet across the bow. That was pretty scary, but not as scary as the time I was reading "The Exorcist," by William Peter Blatty. I can't recall the exact scene at the moment, but I do recall being "very frightened" even as I was reading the book surrounded by other sailors who were also reading. (NOTE: Hard to believe, but when you are out at sea and off duty, you do tend to do quite a bit of reading!)

Another time I was reading "The Shining," by Stephen King. I was at a public pool with about 50 other people. It was the "hallway scene with the Grady twins." If you haven't read the book, you should. And you WILL be very frightened when you get to that section!

So, put on your brainstorming hat, and list a book (or two) or a movie (or two) that made you scared. And WHY did it make you scared?

Ready, Set, Create!

Creative Challenge #7

What do you see? I see a tree!

Well, I did see a tree in Cape May, New Jersey last year. Within a few moments, I realized I could write an essay about what I saw!

So, take a moment and read my essay, which was published in *The Southern Literary Review*.

Your creative challenge is to look around...and find something that inspires YOU to write an essay.

Ready...Set...Create!

On a recent trip to Cape May, New Jersey, I needed a few moments to get out of the sun. It was a hot and humid day, and the shade from three nearby trees was calling my name. As I stood beneath the center tree, I noticed there were about three dozen assorted carvings on its trunk. Some were the usual "MJ loves TR" type of carvings, but others were simply single letters. I wondered whether their carvers had not found true love just yet.

I must also confess that I had no idea what kind of trees they were. Unless I see a palm tree, a Christmas tree or a tree with an apple on it, I'm stumped (pun intended!) by tree identification. My wife is an expert in all things pertaining to gardens and nature, so when I asked her if she knew what they were, she replied, without any hesitation, "crepe myrtles."

According to Southern Living Magazine, "the crepe myrtles are among the most satisfactory of plants for the South: showy summer flowers, attractive bark, and (in many cases) brilliant fall color make them year-round garden performers."

There's no mention of how many of these trees around the country find them-selves on the receiving end of pocket knives, engraved with strange messages that are important to the person doing the carving but cryptic to everyone else. I wondered who was the first person to carve initials or symbols onto a tree trunk?

Researchers have been studying tree carvings, also known as "arborglyphs," to understand people, traditions, and cultures. One thing they have discovered is that the lifespan of a messages carved onto a tree correlates with the lifespan of that tree: When the tree dies, so do the messages. In other words, you won't find stumps or rotted wood with arborglyphs on them. The life or livingness of the tree sustains the message.

Recently I came across The New Forest project in the U.K. Apparently, it was designated a national park in 2005 to "protect and preserve it for the nation to enjoy for generations to come." The New Forest project created a searchable database with information regarding the dates, pictures, poems, and royal marks that can be found throughout the special forest.

The "King's Mark," a broad arrow head, is among the most common tree carvings and was used to identify trees reserved for building Royal Navy ships. There are also trees with concentric circles, commonly known as "witch marks," which were carved to keep away evil spirits. During the Second World War, U.S. Servicemen who were stationed at the nearby airfield RAF Stoney Cross were known to have carved their initials and dates of service into the bark.

Horticultural experts caution against carving into trees because of the potential for damage. But that warning falls on deaf ears. People will continue to carve their messages into trees. I am certain social media will abate this practice. After all, isn't it easier to pull out your pocket phone rather than your pocket knife to confess your love?

Creative Challenge #8

Write a humorous essay!

Many years ago, I worked as a payroll clerk for the Dupont Company in Delaware. I took a bus into town, and while the ride into work was uneventful, the ride home was always an adventure!

I remember one particular bus ride in which some of the other passengers were being obnoxious. I kept my cool, and when I arrived home, I immediately sat down and wrote an essay.

I sold it to Hallmark, and it appeared in one of their gift books, *Laughing Out Loud.*

Enjoy my humorous essay…and then create your own!

"The Commuting Life"

As a commuter on rush-hour buses for many years, I have concluded that although people from all walks of life ride the bus, they fall into four specific categories:

• *Nodders – You can tell these folks have really worked hard all day (or enjoyed a liquid lunch). As soon as they get settled into their seats, their eyes slowly close, and their heads begin to nod, lower and lower. When the bus goes over a big bump in the road the Nodders snap to attention, as if they had been awake all along. Soon their eyes begin to slowly close again, and their heads droop into what I call a "bowing Buddha" position. Nodders have an uncanny ability to wake up just in time to get off at their regular bus stop. (Avoid sitting by Nodders if at all possible. They often drool!)*

• *Talkers – You do not have to be a regular commuter to know who the Talkers are. From the moment they arrive on their bus until they reach their destination, they never shut up. Typically, even outgoing types avoid Talkers because the topics tend to be less than refreshing: Aunt Maggie's gastric anomaly, Little*

Frank's unfortunate birthmark, or the menu for tonight's dinner. When they get on the bus, they quickly scan the prospects and deftly avoid the Nodders.

• *Complainers – Amazingly enough, Complainers have conspired to ensure that one of their own is on every bus ride, regardless of the city, or the time of day or night! Even in small town America at 2:00 a.m., you might not find a Nodder or a Talker, but there will be a Complainer on board. And they often ride in pairs. Complainers do what they do best: complain about everything: the weather, the bumps in the road, the bus schedule, how they hate their jobs, and what's on television that night. Complainers have been known to purposely seek out Talkers. If you see two people sitting next to each other on the bus, and they are both talking a mile a minute, odds are pretty good it's a Complainer and a Talker. Thank goodness they can only hear themselves talking, which is why they don't mind going on and on and on.*

• *Standers – If you have ridden the bus at all, you have seen a Stander. These poor unfortunate souls who left the office a few minutes late, arrived late at the bus stop, followed everyone else onto the bus...and could not find an empty seat. Of course, the real unfortunate ones are those people who have to sit next to a Stander. Standers almost always have an attitude problem, and they don't mind letting people know that standing is no walk in the park. This is generally accomplished with weapons disguised as very large purses, umbrellas, briefcases, tote bags, and even overcoats neatly folded over one arm. Standers seem to wait until their aggravation reaches a high pitch, and then they shift their weapon from one arm to the other, "accidentally" hitting someone in the head, arm or shoulder (whichever is more convenient.). Nodders should avoid sitting by Standers because being hit in the head by a swinging purse or tote bag is no way to wake up, especially on a bus at rush hour.*

I should know. I am a Nodder (and a former Complainer) who never talks, but occasionally stands!

Ready...Set...Create!

Creative Challenge #9

Write a greeting card!

Do you ever get tired of paying five to ten dollars for a greeting card, knowing full well that the recipient will eventually end up tossing it into the trash a few days after the celebration is over? That was how I felt about a decade ago when I was searching for the perfect birthday card for a relative. There were so many choices and it was taking a long time.

It dawned on me, standing in the aisle of that store, that a large share of the cards I was looking through had probably been created by free-lance writers. I had my "light-bulb moment," and knew that I had come across a new source of income as a writer.

I pulled out my pocket notebook, and started to make a list of the various companies that had greeting cards in the racks. I then started contacting them to request their writer's guidelines.

These days, most greeting cards feature a website link for the publisher on the back. Every single one of the card companies I visit online now have their "writer's guidelines" or "submissions information" listed.

I followed the directions from one company, Leap Greetings, and within a week, I had sold my first inspirational verse (less than 30 words!) for $75. And since they were a new company back then, the editor liked my work so much he gave me an assignment for ten more cards at the same price.

So, put on your brainstorming hat and come up with an idea or two for a greeting card. (Bonus points if you are brave enough to submit it to a card company!)

Ready...Set...Create!

Creative Challenge #10

Write a book review!

When I was in elementary school, I was always the student who was "giddy with excitement" when it was time to do a book report! Sometimes the book report was elaborate, and included illustrations, etc., while other times it was only about a page or so long.

Now, I know what you're probably thinking: "I've seen book reviews on Amazon, and they are only a few sentences long."

And while that is correct, that is NOT the type of book review I want you to write.

Instead, think of a longer book review that you see in The New York Times, The Washington Post, or any other publication or website the still publishes book reviews.

My first byline as a freelance writer was a book review.

After receiving rejection slips for over 3 years, I was about to give up ever getting published.

Then I read an article titled "Paging New Book Reviewers" in the 1977 Writer's Yearbook. It gave step by step instructions on how to get a book reviewing assignment from your local newspaper.

I followed their directions, and within a few weeks I had my first official book review assignment! It didn't matter that I wouldn't be paid...because at the end of the review it would say "John Riddle is a Freelance Writer." I had arrived!

After taking a few nonpaying book review assignments, within a few months I was getting paid to write book reviews for The Washington Post!

So, think about a book you have just read, or would like to read, and then get ready to write a book review. Use other book reviews as your model, and you'll do just fine! (Bonus points if you are brave enough to submit your book review somewhere!)

Ready...Set...Create!

Creative Challenge #11

What are you thinking about...right now?

If you're like most creative people, your mind "tends to wander off now and then..."

So, where is your mind going right now? Are you really excited about the creative challenges so far? Or is your mind on something else?

Write it down...you'll feel better!

Ready...Set...Create!

Creative Challenge #12

Would you rather?

Have you ever seen those questions that say "would you rather do this, or rather do that?" I remember taking some type of test in the Navy that helped them figure out what jobs that would be perfect for you. One question was "would you rather read a book about sailboats, or build a sailboat?"

I didn't have faith in that particular test, which should have revealed that I have no "sense of direction" and "suck at math."

So, what did they do? They sent me to Quartermaster school in Newport, Rhode Island, where I spent six weeks trying to learn about navigation (which had a TON of math involved!).

Your challenge is to decide…

Would you rather go on a train ride to an unknown destination…or read a mystery novel about a passenger in the same predicament? AND WHY?

Ready…Set…Create!

Creative Challenge #13

Invent something new!

Have you ever wanted to invent something new? Or how many times have you seen a new product advertised and thought to yourself "I could have created that!"

Your challenge is to "go wild" and brainstorm a new product that everyone will want to use.

(Bonus points if you can draw it, too!)

Ready...Set...Create (and Draw)!

Creative Challenge #14

Give yourself a nickname!

According to various research online, people have been using nick-names since the beginning of time. Abraham Lincoln was known as Honest Abe, Al Capone was Scarface, and on the TV show *Happy Days*, the character known as Arthur Fonzarelli was referred to as The Fonz.

You get the idea.

So, what would you like your nickname to be? And why?

Ready...Set...Create!

Why?

Creative Challenge #15

What was a favorite store you visited as a child?

Everyone has a favorite store when you're a kid. For me, it was "Sadie's," which was only a few blocks from our house. Sadie was a one-eyed butcher who could swing a mean meat cleaver. Half of her store sold fresh meats and deli stuff, and the other half contained a variety of groceries (milk, bread, etc.). She also had "the best candy selections" and in those days you could bring in an empty soda bottle and get anywhere from 2 to 5 cents (depending upon the size) and use it to buy candy!

So, put on your thinking cap...and write a little about a favorite store you enjoyed visiting when you were growing up.

Ready...Set...Create!

Creative Challenge #16

What's your excuse?

"The dog ate my homework."

That excuse has been used a zillion times in cartoons, sitcoms and funny stories...but I often wonder, "did a dog actually eat someone's homework at one time in history?" And then everyone thought it would be a good excuse to use? Who knows...

In the meantime, your creative challenge right now is to come up with FIVE creative excuses...for why you won't be able to make it to your in-law's house for Thanksgiving!

Ready...Set...Create!

1.

2.

3.

4.

5.

Creative Challenge #17

Color some eggs!

No, I don't mean color some eggs with dye like you do at Eastertime. Instead, find some crayons, markers or colored pencils, and color the eggs below!

Ready...Set...Create...opps...I mean Color!

Creative Challenge #18

Decorate the Christmas Tree!

Hope you didn't put away your crayons, markers or colored pencils just yet...because it's time to decorate the Christmas Tree! (Bonus points if you can draw and color a few presents around it!)

Creative Challenge #19

Describe a Vintage Item!

As time marches on, certain things have been replaced by new and improved things, and those things are no longer needed. For example, until Cell Phones came into existence, it was common to see a "phone booth" on a street corner.

Record players have been replaced by CD players...well, you get the idea.

Here's your creative challenge...describe a phone booth, and what it was used for, to someone who has "never seen one!"

AND, describe a record player (and don't forget to talk about how you had to keep replacing the "needles").

NOTE: If you are under the age of 30, you may have to search online for the information, LOL!

Ready...Set...Create!

Phone Booth:

Record Player:

Creative Challenge #20

Tell us about your favorite vacation spot!

No matter how old you are, everyone has a favorite vacation spot. Mine is Wildwood, New Jersey, a beach town that has something for everyone!

Take a few moments and write about your favorite vacation spot. AND, why is it your favorite?

Ready...Set...Create!

Creative Challenge #21

Write a thank you note...Jimmy Fallon style!

If you watch *The Tonight Show* with Jimmy Fallon, you know that on Friday he usually has a comedy bit in which he writes a few thank you notes. Now, these aren't "normal" thank you notes, but instead, you guessed it, they are comedic in nature.

Here are a few actual examples from Jimmy Fallon:

1. *Thank you, chewing gum, for letting my mouth have all the fun while my stomach is like, "Hey man, what gives?"*
2. *Thank you, emails that say, "You have successfully unsubscribed from these emails," for completely missing the point.*

Ready...Set...Create!

Creative Challenge #22

Create a new breakfast cereal...and an ad to sell it!

Some of the most popular brands include Frosted Flakes, Honey Nut Cheerios, Rice Krispies, Froot Loops, Lucky Charms, Apple Jacks, Cheerios, and Cinnamon Toast Crunch.

Your creative challenge is to come up with a new type of breakfast cereal...and describe it in an ad. (Bonus points if you can also draw the front of the box!)

Ready...Set...Create!

Creative Challenge #23

What was your favorite subject in school…and why?

I remember Senator Tom Carper telling a crowd of students, teachers, parents, reporters and lots of volunteers who turned out to help build the "Dream Playground" project at the Brookside Elementary School in Newark, Delaware many years ago what his favorite subject was in school: *Recess!*

Now, we know he was only joking (we hope!). My favorite subject in school was English. I enjoyed writing stories both in class and at home.

Your creative challenge is to share what your favorite subject in school was…and why!

Ready…Set…Create!

Creative Challenge #24

Name a Rock Band!

Ever wonder how a rock band selects their name? I have always been curious, so a little research online revealed how a few popular rock bands decided on the names:

- The Rolling Stones - The band took their name from the Muddy Waters 1950 song "Rollin' Stone."
- The Beatles - The Fab Four were big fans of the Buddy Holly's backing group called the Crickets, and that's where the inspiration for their name came from.
- Malcolm and Angus Young came up with the band name after their sister saw "AC/DC" on the side of an electric sewing machine, and ended up asking, "Why not AC/DC?"

So, what would you name a new rock band...and why?

Ready...Set...Create!

Creative Challenge #25

If you could turn back time..., where would you go? And why?

"*The Time Machine* is a science fiction novella by H. G. Wells, published in 1895. The work is generally credited with the popularization of the concept of time travel by using a vehicle or device to travel purposely and selectively forward or backward through time."

Can you imagine being able to go back in time?

Well, that's your creative challenge.

Where would you go...and why?

Ready...Set...Create!

Creative Challenge #26

Create a new restaurant!

Have you ever eaten a meal at a restaurant, and wondered if they did things a little differently, they might be more successful?

For example, when our 3 children were young and we ate out as a family, when the food arrived at the table my wife and I spent the next few minutes cutting up their food. Sometimes our food would go cold by the time we were ready to eat. That's when I started to envision a new restaurant called "The Ideal Restaurant" (stop laughing).

I even imagined the host at the door saying something like, "Here at the Ideal Restaurant, we understand that parents want their food to be hot when they eat it. That's why WE cut up your children's food before it is brought to the table!" (Trust me, that would be a big hit with parents!)

So, what would your ideal restaurant be like? Give it a name, and describe what would make it "the best."

Ready...Set...Create!

Creative Challenge #27

If you could travel anywhere in the world, where would you go, and why?

This might be an easy question for some people, and more difficult for others. Would you like to visit Paris, or Maui? Or would you settle for someplace closer to home?

With money and time as no object, if you could travel anywhere... where will you go...and why?

Ready...Set...Create!

Creative Challenge #28

What makes you happy?

The search for happiness is never ending, according to research online. Some people are happy with where they are now, and some people think they will be happier if they get a better job, more money, etc.

And we all know people who are "never happy," no matter what is going on in their lives. (Hopefully, that's not you!)

So, put on your creative thinking cap and share what makes you happy.

Ready…Set…Create!

Creative Challenge #29

It's a beautiful day in the neighborhood!

Do you like where you are living right now? Or are you looking forward to moving to a new neighborhood soon?

Your creative challenge is to describe the perfect neighborhood. What does it include? Does it have walking trails? Are there stores nearby?

Everyone has an idea of their "perfect neighborhood."

Describe yours, and why you include the features you need.

Ready...Set...Create!

Creative Challenge #30

If you could perform in a community theater production, what part would you play?

I have been involved with two community theater groups here in Delaware. I started out with the Reedy Point Players in Delaware City, and eventually started doing plays with God's Power and Light Company in Middletown, Delaware.

And for over a decade I was the Director of the Drama Ministries at Cornerstone United Methodist Church in Bear, Delaware (now known as Christ the Cornerstone). Not only did I perform in a few plays at church, but I also wrote and directed over 120 drama sketches that were performed during the Sunday services.

I have performed in *Mary Poppins, Meet Me in St. Louis,* and a long list of Christmas plays. If you have never been involved in community theater, but have a spark of an interest, I urge you to go for it!

Now, back to your creative challenge.

If you could perform in a community theater production, what part would you play?

Ready…Set…Create!

Enjoy these cartoons to celebrate the 20th anniversary of I Love To Write Day. The first one is from Carolyn Belefski, who creates and publishes original comics and illustrations, including her comic strip "Curls." She is artist of the comic books Black Magic Tales, French Fry Club, and The Legettes. Carolyn is a visual communicator, cartoonist, designer, and illustrator whose credits include work for The Obama Administration White House, Clorox, United States National Archives, and many others. She serves as Washington, DC chapter chair of the National Cartoonists Society and was previously an AIGA DC board member. Carolyn designs and produces wearable art such as bandanas, buttons, and enamel pins which are available for purchase at www.CarolynBelefski.com.

This next cartoon was contributed by Bob Eckstein, who is a NY Times bestselling author. His new book is <u>The Complete Book of Cat Names (That Your Cat Won't Answer to, Anyway)</u>.

CREATIVE TIPS...

CREATIVE TIP #1

Joyce Marter, Licensed Psychotherapist, National Speaker and Author shares how she is creative:

Tapping into my creativity was a critical component of writing my recent self-help book, *The Financial Mindset Fix: A Mental Fitness Program for an Abundant Life.* Creative thinking resulted in a more engaging, innovative, authentic, and dynamic book. The following are some tips which helped me access my creativity:

- The night before writing, I would do a short meditation and reflection on the piece I intended to write the next day. I set an intention for what I wanted to convey to my readers.
- After a good night's sleep, I would wake up very early and begin writing at 5 am. I found myself to be most creative during this time which is not too far from sleep and deeper connection to the unconscious mind, and before the interruptions and competing demands we each experience during the traditional workday.

- The start of each chapter was a section which shared something deeply personal about the chapter's topic. I wrote these pieces from my heart and soul with vulnerable authenticity. I tried not to edit myself in the process and to get into a flow state of cathartic self–expression. During revisions, I would streamline these sections so they were clearer and more concise.

- Each of my chapters includes an innovative "wheel exercise" which readers use as a self-assessment tool to measure how well they have learned the chapter's lessons. I had great fun working in collaboration with colleagues in brainstorming sessions. Sifting through my ideas with others allowed creative seeds to blossom into exercises that are unique, powerful and transformative. Because I appreciate visuals, I worked with an illustrator to come up with beautiful illustrations for my wheel exercises.

- Because I wanted my readers to be actively engaged with the book, I incorporated a ton of short exercises–everything from empirically supported psychological techniques to journaling prompts. I made them fun and infused them with humor and creativity. I found the book, *POP!: Create the Perfect Pitch, Title, and Tagline for Anything* by Sam Horn to be extremely helpful in coming up with fun titles for chapters and sections.

- Breaking the book writing process into smaller steps, such as creating an outline, fleshing that out, and then tackling sections that were inspiring me was helpful in reducing overwhelm and allowing the creative juices to flow.

- At times when I felt stuck or when my writing started sounding flat and boring, I took a break, got into nature or did something for fun for even a short amount of time. Then I would verbally convey what I was trying to say in a Zoom recording, access the transcript, and then play with the words until the piece felt infused with vitality and passion.

CREATIVE TIP #2

Chris Smith, author of crime and western novels, shares his story of being creative:

For me, being creative is coming up with and then telling a story that I would enjoy reading, in a manner that I would enjoy reading it in. We all have different tastes, but there are hundreds of thousands of people out there who want to hear your story in your voice.

I've written a series of Mountain Man adventures (the Jim Taylor, Mountain Man adventures) and I had to go and do a lot of research on how to survive in the wild, but I really enjoyed it and I feel that it makes my books more believable.

CREATIVE TIP #3

Walt Larimore, MD, Best-Selling Author of 41 books, including his most recent, *At First Light: A True World War II Story of a Hero, His Bravery, and an Amazing Horse,* shares his creativity tips:

Research has shown that the average person's creative output improves by up to 60 percent when walking (either indoors or out), versus sitting. I've found that to be true. An outside walk, when possible, to commune with God and His creation, seems to spark so many thoughts and ideas. I always have a way (small note pad or smartphone) to record the inspiration He gives me.

CREATIVE TIP #4

Dr. Jo Anne White, a #1 International Bestselling Award Winning Author & Speaker, shares what creativity means to her:

To me creativity is an endless opening to treasure, inventions, knowledge and discoveries. When you tap into it, it's magical and opens a connection to something more than just you: an infinite source, beyond the physical realm.

Don't censure your creativity or inhibit the flow of ideas, curves and bountiful ways and directions your creativity leads you. I've learned quite wonderfully that it can take off as if guided by something more than just myself. That doesn't mean you forgo ideas, a vision or a plan of action. You make the final decision once you've breathed it all in.

CREATIVE TIP #5

Steven James is the bestselling author of many award-winning books. His latest book on the craft of storytelling, *The Art of the Tale*, is available now.

He shares his creative method:

An Exit Sign Revelation

While visiting a hotel in Denver a number of years ago to teach at a writing conference, I noticed EXIT signs not only above the exit doors, but also at their base. *That's weird,* I thought. *Why would anyone stick EXIT signs down there? Only someone crawling on the floor would need a sign by the base of the...*

Oh.

I can't be certain of this, but I'm guessing that whoever placed those signs down there probably looked at things through the eyes of someone crawling for safety. I can picture some sign-hanging guy saying to himself, "Hmm... I wonder what would happen if I were actually trying to get out of this hotel in a fire? Well, I'd be on my hands and knees to stay below the smoke..."

And then he crawled down the hallway looking for a door to escape and realized there wouldn't be any way to see the EXIT signs above the doors because they'd be shrouded by smoke. So, he stuck them next to the floor as well.

That day as I stood there beside the stairwell, staring down at that EXIT sign, I had an epiphany. I'd always thought of creativity as the ability to see what no one else can see—to envision the impossible or to imagine something incredible or totally unique. But in that moment, I realized that creativity isn't so esoteric or unapproachable. It's actually within the grasp of each of us. Creativity isn't the ability to see what no one else can see; it's seeing what anyone else would see—if only they were looking from that perspective.

New ideas are born when we view life from a fresh point of view or peer at the world through another set of eyes. Sometimes that means getting down on all fours and looking at the situation from a totally different angle. When you do that, new ideas unfold.

As you consider stories to tell and ideas to share, let me encourage you to crawl on the floor and look around. To see what no one else is seeing. To look at the problem or project with a new set of eyes.

You don't have to be an artist or a poet or a novelist to benefit from this type of exercise. You might be a reporter or a dry cleaner or a carpenter or a sign-hanging guy in a hotel who dares to enter fully into his work and perhaps manages to save the lives of people he will never meet.

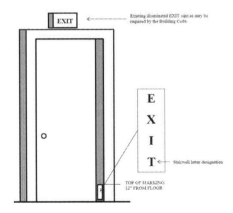

CREATIVE TIP #6

Amanda M. Cottrell, an Art, Mindfulness and Creativity expert, offers her insight into the creative process:

"I guess you are right, I never thought about creativity that way."

This was the response I got after explaining to a parent that their child was unbelievably creative. People often think they are not creative because they felt unsuccessful in the traditional forms of 'creativity' in schools.

When you shift your perception of what it means to be creative you will realize that no matter how much you suck at drawing or painting you are actually infinitely creative too. If you are struggling with contentment and joy in your life then I encourage you to take a step back and reflect on what it is that you truly enjoy doing. You will notice that the things that you got lost in for hours as a child was actually your infinitely creative side expressing itself.

Now that you have an idea of how infinitely creative you truly are, block out some time in your busy day or week just for you. Spend that time truly basking in the joy of the moment and you will see how quickly your soul lights up and you will feel more content and alive.

CREATIVE TIP #7

Leilani Squires is a writer and editor who began working with authors, organizations, and entrepreneurs in 2002. She has a bachelor's degree in Professional Writing from Taylor University and a master's degree in Communications from Regent University.

She shares her thoughts about the creative process:

When it comes to creativity, I remember two quotes. One is from Jack London and one is from a writing mentor of mine. Jack London says, "You can't wait for inspiration. You have to go after it with a club." My mentor said, "We creative people tend to walk this world with our heads tilted ever so slightly. We see the world from a different perspective than everyone else." Creativity isn't something that you can wait on. Just start. It will follow. Write one word. Write three words. Write 200 more! And as you begin, write about what you see from your ever so slightly tilted perspective. The putting together and polishing will happen in your next drafts. Someone out there needs to know they're not alone in their wonderings, confusions, and questions.

CREATIVE TIP #8

Bonnie J. Gibson, a talented author, illustrator and storyteller, shares her thoughts about creativity:

Embracing a Moment...

I love to write. To convey a thought, communicate a moment, weave a message, share some light, inspire a creative spark. Deeply inspired by the limitlessness of adventure, great and mundane. People, nature, animals, loved ones, life. The sharing and togetherness that manifests from the openness. A chance to relish a moment. A chance to assemble and reassemble, with love, hope and purpose.

My own inspiration can spark from something as small as the sound of thunder, a blank canvas, a prayer and just letting the words fly. For me, it is about embracing a moment and discovering if there is more to it. More than what simply meets the eye.

CREATIVE TIP #9

Dr. Carrie Johansson, a psychologist, speaker and author from Denver, reminds us that "we need to be brave!" Her book is *Self Help On The Go,* and she offers her insight into the creative process:

Creativity involves bravery. It is, after all, revolutionary to try something new and different. And it is even more revolutionary to share your creation with the world. I encourage you to notice and then set aside the fear, and put your ideas out into the world. Create and enjoy!

CREATIVE TIP #10

April Tribe Giauque is a ghostwriter, editor, speaker and podcaster from Twin Falls, Idaho. She shares about her own creative process:

What my creative process comes from and feels like...

Thoughts swirling, bubbling, or racing in the river's flow suddenly break free and clamor away. They snag against a low-hanging question I have over the river of my thoughts. I focus on that idea; then, as suddenly as it was snagged, I, along with my captured thought, am released back into the flow of my writing river.

The writing river can then race towards many different parts of the river: intense rapids—spitting and frothing, slow and wide places where a fish of thought will burst through, capturing a bug, or frustrating eddies that seem to hold me forever.

I swirl around and around, trying to write my way out until just as suddenly as I am snagged, I am released at the right time to catch the current and flow of the river again. Timing is always questioned, but it is always right—I trust it more.

As my hands fly across the keyboard, excitement and intense emotions can run high with some writing I do for my ghostwriting clients. Still, it too will pass, and I'll find myself in a deep current being swept downstream and my writing flow pumping out the aftermath of that writing event for chapters and chapters.

Where does the writing process come from?

As a writing professional, words paint images on the canvas of my mind daily. Words are my medium, and they never stop—they are deep within me.

When I am asked to produce writing for an article, a blog, or as a ghostwriter for a client's book, it starts like any mighty river—as a trickle, a creek, or a stream. I never shame how it starts; I am ever grateful that it is there, and I smile at it.

I see the light reflecting off the thoughts and imagery, and then I pool all of that into an *outline* that shapes the banks of the river I'm writing, so I can chart the course of it. I then add a variety of music to it, and I am in writing flow.

As in any great piece of writing, what rapids, snags, and eddies the reader find along the way is the power of the story. But as the creator, I charted the course and put in the time and emotion to feed the flow of thought that created a masterpiece.

CREATIVE TIP #11

Gill James, a writer, editor, publisher and creative writing teacher from Manchester, England shares her thoughts about creativity:

What is it exactly? It was there in the National Curriculum for Modern languages. And then they took it out again because no one could define it. I saw it when a new learner combined something from one module with an item from another and managed to communicate effectively.

What is creative writing? Is it writing that creates something in the reader? Surely that's all writing then? So, studying creative writing means studying what makes writing effective and using that tool.

Constraints lead to more creativity. I was given a list of words, topics and grammatical structures that must be included in the practice German exam papers I was creating. The constraints forced me to write something that the producers of *My Family* might have liked.

Plotter or panster - and are these two creatures really different for you will share an experience; characters and story lines will seem to take on minds of their own.

Creativity is problem solving. The answers come not as we sit at our desk and grapple with the issues, but as we step on to a conference jolly bus, when the apple falls from the tree or when the bath water overflows. For the modern writer it is often as we drive home in the dark, cook a meal for our families or put in the lengths at the swimming pool. There we find our eureka moments.

CREATIVE TIP #12

Laura Schaefer, ghostwriter and author of several dozen books, including the new novel for young readers, *A Long Way from Home*, offers her vision about creativity:

Like many others, I write to find out what I believe. There are moments when the words that appear on the page amaze me. It's the main way I've found to connect with the source energy all around us, the energy that creates life and reveals truth, beauty, pain, meaning.

Of course, not every day of writing is like this. Sometimes, it feels like a pointless and frustrating slog. But I keep showing up because there are days and moments when the words simply flow as if from a divine river. These are the most special moments of life because they are the connection, the reward for participating in the constant unfolding of the universe.

It's my small way of being part of a greater whole. And every time it happens, I am so grateful to be alive. That, to me, is the essence of creativity and I hope everyone can experience it in their own way."

CREATIVE TIP #13

Here's some great info from Adrian Zupp.

G'day! I'm an Aussie expat living in the Boston area. I've been a writer for over 20 years. These days I concentrate on fiction and I have my first U.S. book coming out October 15. It's called *All of My Friends Died in Plane Crashes – Fair Dinkum Stories About Wild Aussie Boys (And a Few Wild Sheilas)*.

I write because I "like the ride," and not for money, or acclaim, or for an agent, publisher or an audience. I write very fast; quite close to "first thought, best thought," because I don't want to disrupt the natural flow of "what's coming out of me" with polish or artifice.

Hence, a prominent bestselling author said that I "write like a house on fire!"

I want my work to be honest and pure, so it is usually just the first draft with minor fixes and a thorough proofreading. I think there is a big difference between a writer and a storyteller. I also believe there's a big difference between writing and simply producing a book. I don't write at a set time; I write when the juices are flowing.

CREATIVE TIP #14

Rowena Roberts, from Stockport, England, offers coaching and courses to help writers tap into what she calls their "authentic creativity." She offers some valuable info on the topic of creativity:

Intentions are magical. They can shape our creativity in ways that we can't even imagine when we first set them.

This is because creativity is more than a skill we can develop; it is a life force that we all have access to. Humans are naturally creative beings; it's what we do. Often, however, we use this force unconsciously, in reactive ways, according to habits and patterns that we have established over many years.

Intention helps us to take our power back and direct our creative life force with conscious awareness and focus. Approaching life with creative intent is to be open to its possibilities, to be curious about how you can connect with it, and to take inspired action as a result of your experiences of it.

Think carefully about intentions for your writing, therefore, as they can change everything.

For example, "Write a novel in one year," may sound like the perfect intention. But what if, after 12 months, you're unhappy with your finished novel? What if, instead, you were nowhere near completion, but you were so much more in love with the novel's premise, characters and the sense of cohesion that it now has; wouldn't you prefer that outcome?

The right intentions bring clarity, momentum, growth, and that all-important touch of magic.

There are all sorts of questions you can ask yourself to set a suitable intention, but here are three simple ones to get you started:

- Why do you want to write?

- How would you like to feel about your writing?

- What impact would you love your writing to have on others?

Look at your answers to these questions and consider: how could they influence what you do when you sit down to write?

And that's it: you're on the path to creative change. Enjoy the journey!

CREATIVE TIP #15

Marina Oksengorn works in the behavioral health field, and offers her insight into the creative process:

I like to write early in the morning on my patio, overlooking the lake, with a cup of coffee nearby. Breathing in the fresh morning air and inspired by the stillness of the day, yet to reveal itself. I challenge you to find a similar spot in your living space and turn it into a daily ritual.

CREATIVE TIP #16

Judson Somerville, MD, Author of the award-winning book *The Optimal Dose: Restore Your Health with The Power of Vitamin D3*, offers a unique perspective on the creativity:

I love the creative process, and when I write about vitamin D3, it is as if the angels are talking to me. I experience a sensation when I start writing like that Amadeus Mozart was shown to experience in the movie "Amadeus." It is almost as if a valve opens, and I feel a rushing sensation and the words just come to me. Like listening to a concert.

CREATIVE TIP #17

Jennifer Brown Banks, a very talented writer and recipient of the 2020 Spirit Award from the Chicago Writers Association, believes in the power of creativity:

Words have magic. As writers, we have the ability to use them to transform, transcend, provide time travel, and share truth with readers.

Never miss an opportunity to share a little magic to make the world better!

I love to write!

CREATIVE TIP #18

This creative inspiration comes from Stephanie Buckwalter, a freelance writer and author from Virginia. She still likes to use paper and pen when the ideas are flowing.

A coworker once described my brain as a relational database—with a random generator. That's probably a good way to describe my creative process, too. My brain sparks ideas all the time. The ones I like, I try to capture on paper. I almost always use paper and pen. That way I can add notes over time and draw lines to link those random thoughts together. As the idea matures, I'll rewrite the idea in a new way and do that as many times as needed until I can work it into an outline. Only then do I hop on the computer and start writing.

Creativity comes in both small and large packages. The smallest detail, like choosing the perfect word or turn of phrase to convey your meaning, can take just as much creative energy as outlining your whole novel. Don't despise the small bits of inspiration. It is often those very small sparks that end up connecting with your reader.

CREATIVE TIP #19

This tip comes from bestselling author Gail Pallotta. Her books are filled with romance, mystery, inspiration and humor.

Any ability I have to create comes from the Lord. Things that have inspired me to write books are a desire to help people and to provide an avenue for readers to escape, to have fun or solve a mystery. Sometimes an incident or incidents rattle around in my head, such as the situations behind *Stopped Cold*. Over the years I crossed paths with quite a few youngsters who suffered because they weren't always winners. When a couple of them ended up with disastrous consequences, it bothered me a lot. Finally, I wrote *Stopped Cold* to say, "You don't have to be #1 for God to love you." My motivation for writing *Barely Above Water* sprang from many people asking about the treatments I received for chronic Lyme disease. With the help of my alternative doctor, I put the facts in a fictitious book. Since I didn't want the story to be heavy material, I added a romance and a rag tag kids' swim team.

My enjoyment of mysteries inspired me to write a couple of cozy mysteries. My mother's beauty shop in a small town where people cared about each other provided the theme for *Hair Calamities and Hot Cash*. *Cooking up a Mystery* started in my mother and grandmother's kitchens, where they created yummy Southern dishes. Strange noises late at night provided the mystery and all things are possible with God became the theme. People create in many different ways—art, crafts, styling hair, helping others with exercise, diet and much more. I'm grateful for the good things the creativity of others brings to my life and hope mine contributes in some way to theirs.

CREATIVE TIP #20

Dr. Jaime A.B. Wilson is in the process of writing his first book. He shares his perspective on the creative process:

Creativity in writing is something that comes over time. There are days when creativity is lackluster. This is normal and all part of the writing process! Don't let the lack of creativity frustrate or deter you. Keep plugging away and give it your best, day by day. Somewhere in those minutes, hours, and days of persistence, creativity will show up with its stunning vistas and beautiful views!

CREATIVE TIP #21

Lucinda Sage-Midgorden, a writer, novelist, blogger and podcaster from Arizona believes we are all creative in one way or another.

I think creativity is part of human DNA. We're all creative in one way or another. The word creativity is often reserved for the arts, but someone might be a genius at revamping business practices so the business runs more efficiently, or they could be a great cook, gardener, or parent. My father had a talent, working with machines. He even invented a tool for use at the submarine base he worked at. He was also a genius at understanding human beings. I used to tell my students that everyone has a genius and it was their job to discover what theirs was.

CREATIVE TIP #22

Margie Goldsmith's stories have taken her to 143 countries on seven continents and have earned her 100 writing awards. Her latest book is *Masters of the Harmonica: 30 Harmonica Masters Share their Craft.* This year she also wrote ten blues songs and recorded them with Rick Esrtin and Kid Andersen at Greasland Studio, San Jose. She also played the set live with Rick Estrin and the Nightcats band at the Red Lion in NYC.

When not writing, traveling, or exploring Central Park, she bikes, hikes, and practices blues harmonica. When visiting foreign countries, she gives away Hohner harmonicas to school children because, Goldsmith says. "Music is a universal language, an ideal way to communicate with everyone, It's my passport to the world."

Here's her view on creativity:

What inspires my creativity is slowing down and giving myself time to digest the silence. If I'm stuck in a rut, my motto has always been "move a muscle, change a thought." So, I'll go to a serene place, which for me is Central Park in NYC where I can hear the wind rustle through the trees and listen to the birds. Or I'll go around the corner to a little "pocket park" which has a waterfall. The sound of water always calms me down and energizes my deepest passions — or if you want to call it "muse," fine.

CREATIVE TIP #23

Barb Eimer began writing for magazines and newspapers in 2002. She has written three books, *Well Loved: Just as I Am*, *All My Favorite Colors Are Red* and *All My Favorite Heroes Are Dead*. She started a business and even traveled across the country in an RV. She considers herself a fun loving, creative problem solver who gets the job done.

Here's what she says about getting into the "creative zone."

I buy fun coffee mugs about writing! One says: "I write. What's your superpower?" A second has the first lines from dozens of famous books.

Another mug I am really proud of says: And then God said, "Let there be sexy people" so he made writers.

I know it's silly, but these mugs give me a little boost of confidence that, heck yes, I'm a writer, so sit down and write something magical!

CREATIVE TIP #24

This next creative submission comes from Kreista Grace, a writer and director who has worked with some of the top names in the entertainment world, including Billy Joel, Elton John, Rod Stewart, Tim McGraw, Faith Hill and many others. (Expect to see three feature films she has written coming to a theater near you in the next few years!)

I love to write because it brings clarity and grounding to my day. The joy I receive while writing my film scripts is expounded knowing others will laugh at the same lines. We share the best of our creativity through our writing to bring joy to others. That's my intent as I write.

When I need to freshen my perspective, I create by speaking a six-line poem, not to be kept, just to be enjoyed in the moment.

CREATIVE TIP #25

Terry Tbone Rhodes, a multi-talented singer, songwriter, actor and director from Florida, is not afraid to face the creative process head on.

For me, creativity happens in its own time and space. As a songwriter/scriptwriter/entrepreneur, most of my best lyrics/thoughts happen when I'm on my motorcycle, or wake up at 4 in the morning to pee. My brain then goes into creative overdrive and I end up having to pull over and capture it before another inspiration takes over and 4 in the morning turns into 6 in the morning. Anyway, it happens. I love it when the creative juices flow.

CREATIVE TIP #26

Alyssa Berthiaume, a ghostwriter, writing guide and the author of *Dear Universe, I Get It Now*, offers some words of wisdom about creativity.

Find a writing practice and schedule that works for you and feels realistic to your goals and schedule. We don't all have to get up at 5 a.m. and burn midnight oil like the greats of the past or commit to thousands of words a day. You'll find more joy in your writing practice if you create a routine/habit/practice that works within the reality of your life. You don't have to write every day or for long hours in order to be consistent, or to strengthen your writing skills.

Since we often don't have available time every day or for maybe not for long periods of time, consider a 'writing sprint.' Put 15-minutes or 30-minutes on the clock and just write. Don't censor yourself or edit every single word. Just get words down on the page. Write. Be proud that you wrote. And when the timer goes up, leave yourself on a little cliff hanger so when you sit back down you can jump back in where you left off.

CREATIVE TIP #27

Gail Wagner is a producer, director, actor, and writer who loves the theater and filmmaking. I first met Gail when I auditioned for a part in a Christmas play for the Reedy Point Players, a community theater group in Delaware City, Delaware. Her perspective on the creative process is very interesting:

A story has to speak to me in some way for me to want to bring it to life on stage or film. I am always amazed how someone takes and idea and puts it on paper. Our job as a director and actor, is to then make it almost tangible for the audience. When acting, I do a lot of research on a character, if historical, as to what it was like during their time period. If biographical, I try to get an insight into the person. I make a biography of the character so that it makes the person 3D. I usually ask my casts to do the same. In "Twelve Angry Jurors," each juror is referred to by their number, never by a name. I met with each actor individually to talk to them about their character's background and how they saw them. The last question I asked was "What's your name?" This made them real. Even if someone is in the ensemble, they should have a name for their character.

I also use colors in a play/film to denote a mood, feeling, or time period. If the character get darker, so should their clothing. Do they have a revelation? If so, their costume could get brighter (or the lighting can). These are subtle hints for the audience to pick up, subconsciously.

CREATIVE TIP #28

Lynn Santer is an Internationally acclaimed film producer and best-selling author. At the tender age of 9, she sent her first story, "The Magical Scarecrow" to a publisher (who recognized her writing skills and encouraged her to write again when she was "a little older").

She offers some very good creative advice:

Never give up, and never give in!

My writing journey began as an infant with crayons on my bedroom wall. Storytelling was an innate insatiable drive from birth. Quickly, my parents decided to keep me supplied with pens and paper!

I sent my first story to a publisher when I was only nine years ago... in secret! Enterprisingly, I found the address inside my prized "Winnie the Pooh" book and used postage stamps gifted to me by my grandma. Proudly, I popped my masterpiece "The Magical Scarecrow" into a letterbox as mother walked us to the shops. Some weeks later a package turned up addressed to me. My mother was aghast. *Who is writing to my child?* The letter encouraged me to write when I was older as my style was excellent but the content not long enough... and they included a brand new "Winnie the Pooh" book! This caused both my parents to be aghast! *What sort of profession is that?*

To placate my parents, I studied finance and law, but ultimately my creative side burst out. My first bestselling title *Sins of Life* was released in 1999. By 2007, I had become an accomplished author and ghost writer and relaunched "The Magical Scarecrows" (now plural) as social enterprise/philanthropic initiative to say thank you to the universe for my success (much longer story for another time).

CREATIVE TIP #29

K.L. Byles is the author of two novels on Amazon from her "Crow" series. She is an encourager of the self-published, and assists writers as a self-publishing consultant. Here is her sage advice:

My advice to new and seasoned authors is don't be afraid of the blank page. It's not ground in stone. Just keep writing. Worry about the mechanics later and hire an honest, competent editor. Never publish a work before it's professionally edited. Otherwise, you're publishing a draft.

CREATIVE TIP #30

Donna F.G. Hailson is an Author, Journalist, Educator, and Speaker who offers some insight into the creative process.

The War of Art, penned by Steven Pressfield, is a book filled with advice from an artist who well knows and well wages the daily battle that is writing "professionally." In this frequently exasperating and thoroughly incisive volume, I have found much with which to resonate. And, as the mother-in-law of a career Marine, I especially appreciate the author's observations on what he learned as a member of the Corps. Contrary to the popular myth, he asserts, "Marine training does not turn baby-faced recruits into bloodthirsty killers. It teaches something far more useful: how to be miserable."

Pressfield concludes: "The artist committing himself to his calling has volunteered for hell, whether he knows it or not. He will be dining for the duration on a diet of isolation, rejection, self-doubt, despair, ridicule, contempt and humiliation. The artist must be like that Marine. He has to know how to be miserable. He has to love being miserable. He has to take pride in being more miserable than any soldier or swabbie or jet jockey. Because this is war, baby. And war is hell."

Yes, professional writing can feel like the waging of a war, but the hardest-won victories are so, so sweet. Aspiring artists are encouraged to take heart from a deep truth reckoned by W. Somerset Maugham: "by performing the mundane physical act of sitting down and starting to work, he [the writer] sets in motion a mysterious but infallible sequence of events that [can] produce inspiration."

The greatest challenge for me has always been the sitting down. But, once I locate the discipline and sit and put pen to page or fingers to a keyboard or voice to a recorder, I begin to sense the win. Then I find myself able to advance on several fronts (multiple projects) and find clarity with real, hard and fast deadlines...I'm writing and I'm loving it!

CREATIVE TIP #31

Tom Garz, an author and inventor, likes what he is doing and has a few tips on how to be creative.

I'm writing what I know and what I don't know. I'm not a popular writer, but I like what I do and it gives me some purpose.

My tips are...

- Take healthy risks in writing and promotion
- Do what you can each day
- Don't look entirely at how much you're making, but rather switch your thinking to how much you might help someone, somewhere, sometime with your writing

CREATIVE TIP #32

Bruce Pittman, a creative writer, ghostwriter and storyteller from Georgia, offers a unique perspective on the topic of creativity. His latest book, *Road to Chiron: Discover the Way to Peace and Joy,* is available on Amazon.

As I think about creativity, the main idea that comes to me is the necessity of being open to new ideas. I am continually watching videos or reading material about innovation or new ideas in various areas such as art, architecture or design.

Also, be patient. My mind moves slow. But it moves deep. So, for me, creativity is something that percolates over time. I don't usually have flashes of creativity. It is usually more like a slow-moving thunderstorm.

So I have learned to watch, listen, and pay attention to what is going on.

For me, creativity will open up in writing when I do the opposite of what is expected. For instance, have you ever noticed on sitcoms that the characters make the worst choices? They do the opposite of what a logical person would do. Of course, it's hilarious. So, I ask myself when developing a storyline - what is the opposite response?

CREATIVE TIP #33

Eddie Jones, author, mentor, writing coach and pirate, has written many books, including an award-winning series of children's books known as *The Caden Chronicles*. Those novels are fun, fast reads for boys who don't like to read. I have known Eddie for a number of years, and if you are looking for a writing coach, he's your guy.

Creativity comes on clouds. Like, three days ago Alfred Hitchcock, with his lower lip poking out, hovered over Lake Norman.

Other times creativity comes by water while surfing or swimming in a lap lane. The comment from a friend can spur creativity. Recently a woman I met commented on a couple who'd agreed to divorce. The pair decided to wait until the end of summer to split because they could not agree on "boat custody." That sent us down a quick but fun conversation of how their story could become a Hallmark movie.

Opening scene in the Spring, they're at the dock agreeing to split. Scenes later, each meet someone else. This leads to their new love journeys. Over the summer, though, the pair must deal with the boat. Keep it afloat, its prop unfouled, cushions cleaned, tank filled . . . metaphors galore spun from those brief comments we discussed.

End of summer arrives and it's time to draw up papers to sell the vessel and split the proceeds. Of course, because it's Hallmark, they can't sell. In working to keep their boat afloat, they have fallen back in love and realized boats and marriage take lots of hard work, money, and time. They reconcile. With her leaning against his shoulder, they decide to take the boat out for a sunset cruise but at that moment it sinks at the dock. "At least we have each other," he says to her. "And we can always buy another boat," she says. "I can never get another you."

Creativity comes when we're watching, listening to others, paying attention to our surroundings. If you're a writer, creativity is never far away. We simply need to move slower sometimes so it can catch us.

CREATIVE TIP #34

Alice Wisler, author and grief-writing instructor, shares what inspires her to write. Her book is *Getting Out of Bed in the Morning: Reflections of Comfort in Heartache.*

A little bald-headed boy, my own, who lived a life of kindness and love and died at age four from cancer-related treatments has held the biggest impact on my writing. The lessons from Daniel greet me each day and fuel me with the motivation to create.

CREATIVE TIP #35

Diana Kelly Levey is a freelance business owner, author and freelance course instructor on Teachable.

What sparks creativity?

For me, exercise gets the creative juices going and helps clear my head if I'm feeling stuck with a freelance assignment or writing a blog post for my site. Lately, I listen to business podcasts and podcasts for free-lancers, and find myself taking a break on my walk with my dog to jot ideas down in my Notes tool. Getting my blood pumping out in the sunshine with some fresh air always does the trick to make me feel like I'm ready to get back to work.

CREATIVE TIP #36

Jennifer Fraser is the bestselling author of *The Bullied Brain: Heal Your Scars and Restore Your Health, Teaching Bullies: Zero Tolerance on the Court or in The Classroom* and *Be A Good Soldier*.

Creativity for me as a writer takes many forms, but all of it is in response to the world we live in. I can be galvanized by a landscape, complex community, striking social-emotional crisis, values-driven conundrum, or a desire to see positive change in our society. I feel gratitude for the immense resources I find in my brain. It's jam-packed with ideas, images, characters, dialogue, scenes and an overall desire to be a story-teller. As a teacher for years, I tried to foster an excite-ment and curiosity in my students when it came to literature and art of all forms. I love the way it enhances our complex empathy.

CREATIVE TIP #37

G. Connor Salter is an award-winning writer and editor from Colorado. He has reviewed over 300 books for various freelance publications, and created weekly articles on pop culture topics.

"Creativity: Opening the Box"

In my mind, I often think of creativity as a magic box. I would approach it gently, tap its fluorescent lid, and gaze into its see-through walls. Story worlds the size of neutron stars. Characters form and reform like quicksilver. I rub my hands, lift the lid, and pull something out of the box like a magician displaying his latest wonder. In real life I find creativity is approaching my computer on a Tuesday morning, the same way I do every morning. I feel feeling annoyed when the screen takes its time switching from void black to fluorescent white. Then I gaze at my dozen half-finished projects in different file folders.

I realize two things. First, I'm not sure which story or character to tinker with next. Second, even when I finish my tinkering, the wonder I felt when sculpting the project in my head won't match the reality once it's finished. Creativity feels magical in the planning stage and the first draft, less so several drafts later. Yet every time I close the computer's lid and get up to find something better to do, I see the ideas in my mind. They will stay there until I get to work. The magic box won't open unless I strive to open it, to understand its contents. Once I've pulled something out of the box, polished it, and released it, the wonder may never match the initial magic in my mind. Still, I will always feel more for a finished project than I feel when I never finish something.

CREATIVE TIP #38

Lisa Pellegrene wears many hats, including author, writer, publisher, film and television agent, animal welfare advocate and Founder of The Sunshine Shop.

I've been writing for as long as I can remember. I've had a lot of inspiration. As a very young girl, I was writing letters to communicate with a pen pal in Australia. She was a little girl named Cheri who my grandma found for me. What a unique and beautiful thing to do I have always thought, as I reflect back. She wanted me to make a true friend, to write back and forth with someone and to expand my horizons, to form a friendship with someone who was from another part of the world.

Another grandma gave me a gift around the age of 10, which I have cherished forever. It was a green paperback book titled, "College Vocabulary," which she found at a local neighborhood sale. I remember asking, "this says 'College Vocabulary' do you think I can learn this? I'm only 10." My grandma said, "I know you can," and I said "okay, great," or something very similar! And that was it. I started to learn college level vocabulary. Now, when I get into a heated discussion with someone, I don't swear, I pull out the "big words," that's when someone knows that they have ruffled my feathers. "Oh, my there she goes, ready to prove a point," they say.

Funny, yes in that regard, but do I immensely value the book that my grandma gave me at a young age, encouraging me to reach higher, strive for more than I fully realized I was capable of at the time, and greatly expand my vocabulary. I most definitely do appreciate this, very much so, every single day. That was a beautiful gift, a gift that keeps on giving.

When I started writing one morning, several years back, I remember waking up that day with so much gratitude - fully knowing that I have a responsibility and purpose to help others more, given my inspiring and beautiful life lessons; well, this knowing and taking action to begin to write is what led to my book *Be Epic, Choose Love.*

I simply started writing and the words flowed naturally like a river!

I didn't know that I was writing a book until I was about 60 pages into it, and then it dawned on me - this is a book to help encourage others, heal hearts and to inspire love. It was my mom who encouraged me to keep writing. She was the only person who read some of what I wrote initially and her response was "this is beautiful, honey - keep writing." And so I did.

Truly loving life and living life, and being fully present for each precious moment inspires me. And valuing each and every moment, as this gift of life continues to unfold. I write to encourage others, and I write to inspire love, hope, truth, empathy and compassion in a world that so very much needs all of it.

CREATIVE TIP #39

Judy Colbert is a freelance writer, author and photographer from Maryland. Her latest books include *100 Things To Do In Baltimore Before You Die* and *Virginia Off the Beaten Path: Discover Your Fun.*

I'm naturally curious. I think most good journalists are. When I see something interesting, I'm vain enough to think others will agree with me, so I research and write about it. I love when someone says, "I never knew that. Thanks for letting me know."

CREATIVE TIP #40

Deborah Hunt is an experienced academic administrator, nurse educator, writer, researcher and author. Some of her books include *Hannah and the Hobgoblins, No Dinosaurs Allowed* and *The One-Eyed Pig.*

Books and writing have always been my passion. The books that were read to me as a child and eventually I read on my own inspired me to be a writer. I am eclectic so there are many things that inspire my creativity. I write every day and keep a journal. Journaling has served as a source of reflection and has improved my ability to put my thoughts onto paper which is not most often on my laptop. My ideas come from my life experiences with my family and friends, the places I have visited, and people I have met in all different settings.

Writers usually have excellent observational skills which provides a constant source of potential stories and characters. These experiences may be mundane and quite ordinary or unique and extraordinary. Immersing myself in these experiences using all five of my senses truly inspires my creative writing process. For example, when I am at the beach (one of my favorite places to write) I close my eyes and think about how the spray of the saltwater feels like a fine gentle mist among the aromas of salt, sand, suntan lotion. The sun rays enveloping me like a warm blanket. As I open my eyes, I see the beautiful white and gray puffs in the sky and imagine what it would be like to float on one of those clouds.

Sometimes the clouds are shaped like a dragon or puppy, and I think about possible stories. The sand feels warm and silky to touch and I think about other types of sand I have walked on and what were the people like who walked these same sandy beaches one hundred years ago. What will the future look like? How will erosion change the shape of the beach and bluffs. I listen to the chatter of the sunseekers while observing their attire, their beach umbrellas, chairs, beach toys, and colorful towels. One or more of these people may become the inspiration for one of my stories. I watch the waves crashing on the surf taking everything in its path to the shoreline and just as quickly back to sea. I observe the remnants scattered along the surf while seagulls fly overhead in search of a tasty treat. Will they be part of a future story? Your life experiences can be the inspiration for a future story or character. You just need to learn how to immerse yourself in the experience, use your senses, and write them down in your notebook or journal.

CREATIVE TIP #41

Dr. Kristen Lee, a.k.a. "Dr. Kris," is an internationally recognized, award-winning behavioral science clinician, researcher, educator, speaker, author and comedian from Boston, Massachusetts. She is the host of "Crackin' Up: Where Therapy Meets Comedy," and is a regular contributor to Psychology Today and other publications.

Reading and writing are my air. Creativity is one of my deepest held values, and my daily practice of writing is truly something that elevates and nourishes me. As an artist, I am able to create psychological distance from that which haunt and compromises my spirit and well-being. Creative expression is truly a way we can liberate ourselves and one another, the very reason we are all here!

CREATIVE TIP #42

Julie Burnett is a talented writer from Arizona, and says that "writing saved my life."

Writing saved my life.

I started writing and daily journaling seven years ago on Christmas morning. I wrote down my thoughts and feelings. I was struggling with a lack of self-worth. Why am I all alone on Christmas? No one must want me. I must not be good enough. No one cares about me. Does this sound familiar?

Later, I was able to read what I had written about myself. I was eventually able to see myself as others saw me. I wrote all the negative thoughts down on paper. I got those thoughts out of my head. I stopped the repeating negativity that had played over and over in my head. I didn't really believe I was any of those things. That broken record was learned over many years growing up in an abusive and dysfunctional household.

I began to rewrite my story. Changing my words to reflect positivity and who I really was inside. By looking at what I had written, I was able to see myself as others do. I'm highly intelligent. I'm attractive. I'm healthy. I'm strong and independent. I learned it's ok to be vulnerable. It's ok to cry. I love myself. I cut myself breaks. I let go of the haters and focused on myself rather trying to change others. I appreciate differences more than similarities. I don't waste all my time on social media. I know me. The real me. That it is ok to just be me. I couldn't see me, until I started to write.

Writing heals the soul. Writing heals the wounds. All this for the cost of a pen or pencil and paper. You don't need a computer or expensive software. JUST WRITE IT! KEEP WRITING!

CREATIVE TIP #43

Andrea Merrell is an author, professional editor, workshop leader and mentor. Her passion is to encourage other writers, helping them to sharpen their skills and polish their prose. She is a wife, mother, grandmother of six, a Hallmark mystery movie junkie, and lover of coffee and dark chocolate.

Her books include *Murder of a Manuscript, Praying for the Prodigal* and *Marriage: Make It or Break It.*

As writers, we're always looking for inspiration. Creative ideas. Anecdotes. Good hooks. Stories to encourage and inspire our readers. God is the master of creativity, and He imparts that gift to us when we look to Him.

Inspiration is all around us. Nature. People. Children at play. Hard times and even tragedies. Sickness. Unexpected blessings. It might come from our home, our workplace, the grocery store, a hike in the mountains, or a day at the beach. It might come when we're watching a sunset, having our quiet time, or watching a silly sitcom on TV.

Approach your writing as you approach your day—in response mode to the giver of life and the maker of all things. Be on the lookout for all He is doing … in, through, and around you. Let Him be your inspiration. He will never let you down.

CREATIVE TIP #44

Dr. Todd P. Kashdan is a Professor of Psychology, a leading educator to the public and the author of five books, including *Curious? The Upside of Your Darkside* and his latest title, *The Art of Insubordination: How to Dissent and Defy Effectively*. He gave a TEDx talk on psychological flexibility and writes the "Curious?" blog for *Psychology Today*, which is enjoyed by more than four million readers.

If you are going to be a writer, you have to stop whenever the inspiration hits. This means pulling the car on the side of the road and jotting in a notebook. If you wake up at 3 a.m., you push through the pain and get those words or images down and then crawl back into the sheets. You never know when the ideas swirling between outside influences and internal experiences rear their head.

CREATIVE TIP #45

Deb Haggerty is the Publisher and Editor in Chief at Elk Lake Publishing in Massachusetts.

What some people view as creativity is often the result of years of studying the craft, writing, rewriting, getting rejected over and over, until one day, THE idea hits and success follows. Hard work + practice + continual learning may = success!

CREATIVE TIP #46

Sherry Fink is an Inspirational Speaker, a Bestselling Children's Author and Founder of Whimsical World, an empowering brand whose mission is to inspire, delight and educate children of all ages while planting seeds of self-esteem and high achievement. Some of her books include *World Of Whimsy With the Little Unicorn*, *The Little Penguin* and *The Little Monster*.

When deciding whether or not to go for your dream, remember that you don't need a bigger net, you just need bigger wings!

CREATIVE TIP #47

Lady LeeAnn Roberts of Glencoe is an author from Glasgow, Scotland. She believes music is everything, and says she can't go a day without listening to it, and its constant spurs of inspiration for her writing.

It is said everyone has a book inside them, but that's just not true. They may have a story to tell but writing and editing is extremely hard. It is not called a craft for no reason and it's something you must work at constantly. You need a great vocabulary so you're not using the same words over and over. You will have to understand grammar before you even begin to learn to write. For instance, who vs whom and when to use them, and the most mistakes for there, their and they're.

That's not even starting on all punctuation rules. There are so many mistakes an untrained writer will make and not even know it. So much blood, sweat and tears go into writing a book as you write the first draft quickly whilst the ideas are still fresh, then you have go bend it, twist it, break it and shape it until it is your original vision on the page. Study the craft of writing and you must read a lot, good books and bad to compare the different kinds of writers. Basically, writing is a lot of work behind the scenes in the form of research and notes before you even write a word. That being said, I love to write and create characters and their worlds and stories. I believe writing is a calling, not just a job.

CREATIVE TIP #48

Mark "Cap'n Slappy" Summers is one of the two creative geniuses behind the "International Talk Like A Pirate Day," which is celebrated every September 19th. Fun fact: In 2002, the same year I launched "I Love To Write Day," bestselling humor author and syndicated columnist Dave Barry wrote an article about the Pirate Day. Dave actually wrote a very funny piece, and poked fun at the idea. The next thing you know, "International Talk Like A Pirate Day" is everywhere! (I have written to Dave Barry a few times, asking him if he would write a humor column about ILTWD, but so far, he has declined.)

Ahoy John,

My creative process starts with an openness to and fascination with the mundane - finding new perspectives and reframing those things that we see every day. For example, most of my entries on The Face-books start with, "Napoleon's notes on this morning's walk." As we walk around our town, I try to think of how my pit bull, Napoleon, would make sense out of the things he sees and I write in what I would imagine would be his "voice." One Saturday morning as we walked through Bryant Park, we saw a Little League baseball game being played by adolescents. Napoleon heard the sound of the ball clinking off a bat an referred to it as, "clinksclub," and didn't know the name for what he called, "elder hooman pups," so he called them, "indolescents."

So, for me (and Napoleon) it's all about thinking about things we know - but differently.

CREATIVE TIP #49

Jacob Nordby is the President and Co-Founder of the Institute for Creative Living. Their mission is to assist people as they heal and strengthen the connection to their inner creative selves. He is also the author of *Blessed Are the Weird,* and *The Creative Cure.*

You know how every once in a while, you do something and that little voice inside says "There. That's it. That's why you're here." And you get a warm glow in your heart because you know it's true. Do more of that.

CREATIVE TIP #50

Erika Sneath is a very talented children's book author, Academic Dean & Curriculum Specialist and a very creative person. Her book, *Adalene Plays Many Ways*, will be published in November of this year.

When I envisioned writing my own children's book, I assumed it would be loosely related to school in some way. I had pictured it going on the recommended books in my own classroom library, and sharing it with all of my students. What I didn't anticipate is suffering from an injury that resulted in me experiencing chronic pain. This is ultimately what I chose to write my book about. I share this to remind any fellow readers and future writers that your story is out there! Draw from your own experiences. Think about what you're passionate about. What do you hope your own kids, family members, neighbors, and the greater community take away from your story?

For me, the creativity flowed as soon as I thought through the above questions. And, I also wasn't ready to answer them for several years. Find the happy medium between pushing yourself outside your comfort zone and waiting until you know your purpose. It's out there!

CREATIVE TIP #51

Diana Baker is the Co-Pastor, Worship Leader and Teacher at Prayer and Praise Christian Fellowship in Woodstock, Georgia. She is also an extremely talented freelance writer, editor and blogger.

My creativity is sparked when God drops a "golden nugget" idea into my mind, and challenges me to bring it to life!

CREATIVE TIP #52

Broyony Best is a published author residing in the UK. She writes memoir style books that shine a light on Mental Illness, Addiction Recovery and Happiness. Her books are currently being used as mental health resources in the UK and USA, with phenomenal reviews and feedback.

My inspiration for writing hit me like a tidal wave when I was mediating one morning, like a light being turned on that emanated brighter with each idea that entered my mind. My creative process for my first book was to sit at my laptop and just type any thoughts that flowed through, me then left to fill up the screen. For my second book my process was slightly different, as I planned which messages and stories I wanted to share with readers for each chapter, then again, I just let the creativity flow.

If you write about a topic you are passionate about, the inspiration and creativity will never run dry.

CREATIVE TIP #53

Tammy Collins is an award-winning artist, interior designer, brand strategist, marketing consultant, author and publisher who loves to be creative.

Creativity is an expression of your passion. It is not something that only talented or gifted people have or do. Everyone is creative and expresses their passion differently. Some are more creative and expressive than others. Many have not connected to their passions and don't play with their creativity. Many think being creative is solely based in the arts. Visual, performing, music, photography, design, and writing are not the only ways to express creativity.

Gardening, cooking, flower arranging, decorating, crafts, organizing, hosting, communication, journaling, gift giving, teaching, doctors, nurses, lawyers, barista, librarian, hairstylists, dog groomers, athletes, farmers, mothers, fathers, and every interest and career is a form of creativity when it's something the person is passionate about. The way you express your creativity is unique. When your passion aligns with your actions, you are using your creativity. The more you engage your passion, the more your creativity grows. This alignment is the key to being truly happy.

CREATIVE TIP #54

Geri Spieler is an author, internet research expert, experienced newspaper reporter, and former research director.

Being creative as a writer, I find inspiration all around me. I write in several genres; nonfiction, fiction, blogs, books, and articles.

A big part of the creative process for me is in doing research. In fact, I'd have to say doing research is my most creative process next to writing.

It takes every one of my creative bones to find the right questions to ask and get the information I need for the writing process. Conducting interviews is especially creative as you need to know how to listen and when to press for more. Tricky stuff.

CREATIVE TIP #55

Denise Dorman is the CEO of WriteBrain Media, a woman owned award-winning agency. She is a very talented Video and TV producer, journalist and author who has extensive experience as a Creative Director.

I hear many creatives lament "creative blocks," but I don't experience them. I learned a handy life hack for getting past that stuck phase: laughter. When you can access comedy that makes you laugh, it relaxes you. Once you're relaxed, then you can more easily open your mind to think with greater creativity. Some of the touchstones I use include the *Deep Thoughts by Jack Handey* books (he also has a website), the old *David Letterman Top 10 Lists*, or I'll watch a few online clips of standup like Paul Mercurio, Sebastian Maniscalco, Jim Gaffigan, Jim Breuer and Steven Wright.

CREATIVE TIP #56

Dr. Leslie Ellis is a registered clinical counsellor, teacher and author of *A Clinician's Guide to Dream Therapy*.

My dreams are a rich source of creativity for me. The images that come through dreaming are unique and unfettered by my internal editor or critic. At times, my dream images are so strikingly original, they seem to be demanding creative expression. I am not alone in this -- through the ages, dreams have inspired music, art, poetry and invention. As a prompt for writing, they have often helped me think way outside the box, have helped ideas come alive and have pointed the way forward when I've been stuck. I've noticed that dreams help most if you ask them -- so I suggest setting an intention at night to have a dream that inspires your writing process.

CREATIVE TIP #57

Susan Setteducato is an award-winning artist and author of a YA Fantasy Series.

Since I can remember, I've written things down, trying to catch feelings and moods like butterflies. Strings of words sometimes became drawings or paintings, but mostly they turned into poems, then later, scenes in stories. As an adult with three complete novels written and four more brewing, I can look back now and see clearly that all along, I've been mining my own interior. The work is hard, sometimes exhausting, but I am inspired to keep on because I feel nourished by deepening my craft. Writers are in an endless learning curve, which I love because there is no arriving. I love the music in words and the catharsis they can create. In my view, stories can change the world.

CREATIVE TIP #58

Tracy Crump's numerous articles and devotionals have appeared in national magazines, such as *Focus on the Family*, *ParentLife*, *Mature Living*, *Woman's World*, *The Upper Room*, and Guideposts books. She was a columnist for *Southern Writers Magazine* for more than four years and contributed articles to three newspapers. She dispenses hope in her new book, *Health, Healing, and Wholeness: Devotions of Hope in the Midst of Illness*. Incorporating stories from her nursing and caregiving seasons, her book ministers to those facing a health crisis or walking alongside a friend or loved one who is. Churches are using the book as a resource for hospital ministries, community outreach, and pastoral care.

When I write true, inspirational short stories, the first thing I do is read the story callout for ideas. *Chicken Soup for the Soul* and other anthologies often list possible topics that will fit with their upcoming book. Those may spark a memory of something that happened yesterday or something that happened twenty years ago. As a friend said, "Our lives are not one long biography but thousands of little stories." We just have to trigger memories of those stories.

In our workshops on writing for *Chicken Soup for the Soul*, my co-presenter and I often recommend using an idea web. Starting with a broad topic (the book theme), we draw branches to subtopics that we continue to narrow down into subjects that would make good stories for the book. Some will be appropriate, and some won't. But the process gets ideas and creative juices flowing.

CREATIVE TIP #59

Jane Risdon had a career in the International Music business before becoming a full-time writer and author.

I've worked with musicians and writers and I'm of the firm belief that talent is a gift, and inspiration comes from the 'ether.' I don't believe the gift - writing and any other creative talent - can be learned, but I do believe it can be enhanced and honed as any skill can.

CREATIVE TIP #60

C. Hope Clark is an award-winning writer and author of numerous books, including *The Carolina Slade Mysteries*. She also publishes a free weekly newsletter for writers, *Funds For Writers*.

Creativity is an escape from whatever captivity the world imposes upon you, allowing you to be yourself in its deepest, purist, most-unadulterated form. It's you being you, without reservation. Disappearing amidst my words is incredibly cathartic for me, giving me untethered permission to just be myself. Words are my purpose. Words make me feel incredibly whole.

CREATIVE TIP #61

Sherry Briscoe writes suspense mysteries with a flavor of the paranormal. Her childhood heroes were Alfred Hitchcock and Edgar Allan Poe, and she insists that episodes of *The Twilight Zone* made perfectly fine bedtime stories.

With degrees in Journalism, Photography, and Adult Education, Sherry covers all her passions of creativity and teaching others. She lives in the Pacific Northwest with her husband, who keeps her stocked in chai tea lattes and lemon drop martinis, and her Burmese cat, who shares her popcorn, pizzas and even an occasional beer. Sherry is a world traveler, US Army Veteran, and active member of her writing community.

Her creative submission is short and to the point:

I write the story inside of me that wants to be told, not the story I want to tell.

CREATIVE TIP #62

Charlene Redick is a playwright, poet, fiction writer, painter and working artist.

The poet is blessed with the ability to describe what others feel through beautiful language that can move others to tears. In doing this work, the poet takes emotion recollected in tranquility and offers it to the world as a poem. I find that my poems often come from a quarrel with myself, or from world-sickness, love-sickness, a sense of wrong, a lump in the throat.

CREATIVE TIP #63

John Chandler says that his goals are to make cool things that people will love, and he succeeded in many areas, including creating "The Skrumps," presented by The Jim Henson Company.

I discovered the book *Madeline* in my baby sister Hailey's room when I was 22 years old. I was an aspiring stand-up comic and wrote all of my own material and a lot of it was rhyming songs that were funny. I had no formal art training as an illustrator, but I was aware of the *Madeline* book and knew it was famous.

This changed the course of my life because I figured the illustrations were simple and I could learn fast to do drawings as good as the ones in that iconic book.

Soon after realizing this, I sat down and wrote a rhyming storybook that I felt was funny enough to make my friends laugh. It was as funny as the comedy shows I was performing that were getting lots of laughs. After writing this first story I began to illustrate it. I knew the pictures would be rough but it did not matter to me because all of the people that I knew looked at me as a crazy comedic type guy so who cares! The real challenge for me was can I actually finish drawing the whole story without giving up mid-way through.

As it went, I did finish the book, scratching it out with black pens and colored pencils, page by page as fast as I could so I wouldn't lose interest and stop mid way through. Upon completion of my very first picture book

I was so happy. I ran to Kinkos Copies and bound it into a real book and read it out loud to all my friends and family.

Although the book illustrations were clearly amateur, the story was clever and made my friends laugh.

After that I was hooked, and 35 books later (and around 9 years) I had published 8 of my original storybooks, and had my own toy line called "The Skrumps" in toy and book stores. It was made into a digitally animated miniseries with The Jim Henson Company. That's the way I got up on the whole creative writing game.

CREATIVE TIP #64

Scott McConnell is a Story Consultant from Australia who helps novelists, producers and publishers develop story concepts and stories to a professional level.

To be creative I need a relaxed, open mind. That is, to be in a mental space where I am focused and free with the story I am working on. No big outside distractions or problems. Then my subconscious will be best able to answer the questions that I am asking it. Then I can truly be the Muse of my imagination.

CREATIVE TIP #65

Carol Kjar is a retired technical writer/editor who has self-published nine books on Amazon. She loves to encourage other writers, especially those who are just starting out.

Got writer's block? Take a shower. Water has a wonderful way of soothing away distractions and letting my imagination run free. Many a plot hole was filled and story line improved with hot water from a showerhead. Water shortages in your area? Head to the nearest fountain, lake, or river. Let the magic of water inspire you!

CREATIVE TIP #66

Nancy Shenker is in Scottsdale, Arizona, and helps companies transform, re-imagine, and scale. She is an author, brand marketer, innovator, content strategist, creator, and provocateur.

Writing is like breathing to me. I've been doing it since I could hold a crayon. From short poems and fantasy tales to boring financial services copy and e-mails, to thousands of fun articles, 8 books, and a site about dating >50, I have written throughout my life and now make most of my living doing it. I now use my phone or laptop rather than a crayon, but that childlike glee when I look at a blank page (or screen) is timeless!

CREATIVE TIP #67

Karen Bricker is a former early childhood and dance teacher who now practices physical therapy and lives in Southeastern Massachusetts with her husband and kooky, but caring cat, Shadow. Her children's books include *The Magic Straw Hat, Destination Adventure* and *Maddie's Saturday to Remember.*

I am inspired to write children's books to bring imagination and spirit to young readers. When I was young my dad always was ready to explore what could be the next great adventure right around the corner.

CREATIVE TIP #68

Christy Whitman is a New York Times bestselling author and Master Certified Law of Attraction Coach. She offers the "7 Step Process" from her latest book, *The Desire Factor: How to Embrace Your Materialistic Nature to Reclaim for Full Spiritual Power.*

1. *Align with what you want in words, thoughts, emotions, perspectives, and actions*

2. *Focus only on the good and what you want*
3. *Joyfully expect your good to materialize.*
4. *Feel the having of what you desire*
5. *Love the idea and feeling of your desire*
6. *Surrender any resistance to attaining your desire*
7. *Take massive action towards your goals*

CREATIVE TIP #69

Susan Bishop is a feet-to-the-fire certified professional co-active coach who works with entrepreneurs, founders, executives and any individual or organization seeking to "shake mountains." Susan began her career in the creative departments of ad agencies and knows what it's like to put ideas out there. She is a poet, artist and cyclist, as well as a step-mom to two amazing women, and wife to a man who still has no idea what she does for a living.

I never thought much about what I call external creativity saboteurs (a.k.a. others) until I started to put my creations into the world on a regular basis. To support myself in that process, I conducted a survey among my writer friends. I asked them, "What's the most important advice you can offer about sharing your work with others?"

One of the answers I received was NOT what I was expecting. It was: **Protect your creations. With claws and fangs if necessary.**

Gosh, I thought, you're *supposed to* listen to others, you *should* take and even incorporate their feedback. If you don't, you're being defensive, closed, ego-driven – and that is not a great place to be if you want to expand your creativity, right? But in reality, showing an idea too early, allowing too much feedback, being too open to others' ideas can limit your creation from being all it could and even destroy it. We all deserve to give our ideas a chance to develop fully and this one piece of advice has helped me stretch myself and be more prolific for over 20 years.

It's given me space and time to create, freedom to take real risks and it has resulted in work I never would have produced if I hadn't given myself permission to stand my ground, claws and fangs at the ready. Of course, there's a flip-side to this advice that's valuable too. But when it comes to simply getting going and taking your ideas as far as you can, remembering that all creations are fragile at first and desperately need room to breathe can be game-changing. For me, realizing that in the face of "construction criticism" I had the right (and good reason) to say no thanks grew my creative confidence monumentally. I trust myself today because once, a long time ago, I got this very counter-intuitive advice and it has been the gift of a lifetime.

CREATIVE TIP #70

Henry McLaughlin was tagged as "one to watch" by Publishers Weekly. He lives in North Texas where he writes, teaches, and coaches. His stories take readers on adventures into the hearts and souls of his characters as they battle inner conflicts while seeking to bring restoration and justice to a dark world.

What Inspires My Stories?

The most common way I get story ideas is from an image that pops into my mind. Many times, I can't remember what I was doing, reading, or thinking when the idea came to me. I gave up asking myself, "Where did that come from?"

One story I'm working on right now, *Mr. Latham's Lincoln,* is with a prospective agent. The idea came to me over ten years ago. On this one, I remember what I was doing when I received it. I was lying in bed about to go to sleep.

It was the image of a man around sixty years old. He was fumbling to put his cowboy boots on. Then he was fumbling to connect the lights on his flatbed trailer to his truck. He wasn't drunk or under the influence of anything. He was flustered and in a hurry. It was late at night, after midnight. Don't ask me how I knew this. I just did.

The next night, it was the same image. By that time in my writing career, I'd learned enough to know I had to go further with it. The right brain creative side—the boys in the basement, as James Scott Bell calls them—came alive.

"Why is he doing that?"

The answer: It's the middle of the night and he—his name is Charlie—receives a phone call from his adult son. The son's wife's car was found off the interstate in Oklahoma City. And they cannot find his wife. Charlie is hurrying to get there to help his son and is bringing a flatbed trailer to carry the car back.

More questions told me more about Charlie. He's a horse rancher in the North Texas town of Justin. He loves Jake, his only child, and his daughter-in-law, Amy. A strong Christian, he is a rock in his church. His wife left him and Jake 30 years earlier for another man. Charlie never remarried and has avoided serious relationships with a woman like the proverbial plague.

From there, it was, as Faulkner suggests, following Charlie around. What happens? What actions does he take? Why does he do one thing and not the other? It's getting to know Charlie on his terms, on letting him show me who he is through what he thinks, says, and does.

More questions followed:

What does he want? What is his goal? He wants to find Amy and restore her to the family.

What obstacles prevent him from achieving his goal? They find evidence Amy planned her disappearance. Why? What is she running from? Or running to? How does he overcome them?

And the big question: Where is God in all this?

Charlie answers these and other questions over the course of the story. This is where writing by the seat of my pants is fun. Charlie is free to go where his heart and the story lead him.

How about you? What inspires your stories?

CREATIVE TIP #71

Samuel Sanders is the author of *Your Next Big Idea: Improve Your Creativity and Problem-Solving,* and is a "creative wizard!"

When looking to be creative, my first step is examining problems more closely. Most creations are based on solving problems, satisfying needs, or fulfilling wants. So, I'll think about problems I am having or try to notice problems others are facing, and I'll think about what wants I or others have, to see if I can cater to them. If I am really stuck, a good trick is to go for a walk. Sometimes my best ideas come when I am strolling and thinking.

CREATIVE TIP #72

Kathleen Becker Blease is an Ex-Random House Editor, freelance developmental editor and an artist.

Close to my home in a small city on the Delaware River a narrow road twists along the nearest creek, skims against granite and slate walls on the backside of some Pennsylvania quarries, and winds through horse farms, over some topography that welcomes you with grazing cows on the left and a vast flank of wildflowers, amassed with Queen Anne's

Lace, on the right. At its peak, the view lays out a tapestry of knitted rolling hills and, says my friend from Britain, closely resembles Scotland. A few winters ago, an arctic blast swept through the east coast, and this road, my favorite and what people call with affection "the Easton-Bangor highway," turned into a treacherous ribbon of ice the locals warned one another to avoid.

A day had gone by and, not unexpectantly, a man came about with a rig and know-how and cleared it. That's when we discovered that something magical had happened. The bitter cold air of the bracing blast from Canada and the brilliant January sun co-mingled and painted the trees and cut corn stalks and winter wheat and the vestiges of the remaining skeletons of the Queen Anne's Lace with crystalized prisms as far as the eye could see. Colors dancing across the snow-covered hills and the interlocking branches that hung close to the road dazzled those drivers who slowed down to notice, or dared to find a place to pull over to soak in the display of reds and violets and yellows and greens.

If you could hold this in your hands, they would overflow with white diamonds. Even the blue-black granite walls were bejeweled. This, dear reader, is my journey of creating. Particularly, of writing. It twists and turns, runs against both the life-giving water and the hard walls. It blossoms. It injects fears. Sometimes it begs you to stay away. Then it gives a bounty of rewards in the end.

A writer discovers, witnesses, ponders, remembers.

A writer dares to journey and creates something that once didn't even exist.

Something that soothes, or entices; something that fantasizes, or clarifies a reality. Like a memory, written words, your words, possess a certain kind of power. And, published or between the covers of a bedside journal, they will live a very long time.

CREATIVE TIP #73

Nancy Gentle Boudrie is the Founder & President Awaken With Light Inc. For 35 years, Nancy has helped Business Owners and Corporations peak perform and create exponential success. Whether setting up safety programs in the transportation industry, or creating multi-million-dollar independent insurance agencies, one of which was her own, Nancy has been assisting business professionals and organizations in creating seven-figure success.

One of my favorite exercises to do when I am feeling a shift or change, a period of self-awareness that I am going through some growth, is something called "morning pages." This exercise was introduced to me when I interviewed Julia Cameron on my Gentle Power Radio, Voice America Radio Show. The idea is to begin your day writing in a journal whatever comes to mind. These thoughts do not need to be complete sentences; just allow your consciousness to flow out on paper. This exercise can have a profound and transformational impact. So much so that Julia has sold millions of copies of her book *The Artist's Way.*

Expressing myself through writing is not only therapeutic for me but can be where I gain my greatest inspiration. Sometimes I feel God is using me to communicate something to others. This is a process that cannot be forced. I begin by centering myself and connecting to Source, God for me; I imagine each breath I take allows the love and light of the field energy all around me to flow, Awakening the light within me. That light is the 'I am" or God. Then I begin and allow my creativity to flow.

At first it may seem robotic but as I allow just thoughts to flow from me, I can see the art that is being created.

CREATIVE TIP #74

Thomas Smith is an award-winning author whose latest novel, *Something Stirs,* was just released.

Some people confuse creativity with ideas. We have ideas all the time. Everything from an idea for a new novel to thinking about having spaghetti for supper. In fact, try NOT to have an idea. It's almost impossible.

Creativity happens when you ACT on the idea. That's when the creative process really begins. It's not magic. It's work. You sit down at the computer and begin to type. You gather the ingredients for that pot of spaghetti sauce. No matter what you do, the creativity comes from the work itself. Maybe you make the sauce the same way you have for years. It doesn't matter. You took the ingredients and combined them to make the perfect sauce for the pasta. And if in the process you decide to add a new ingredient, you're still creating. The same goes for writing. You can have all the ideas you want, but the magic happens when you begin to type. No matter what kind of writing it is, when your finger touches that first key, the creativity begins!

CREATIVE TIP #75

Nanette Saylor founded Wise Well Women to support worn-out women and high-achieving women who were itching to create something more purposeful and joyful in their lives. It's her deepest desire to be a beacon of light for you as you embrace your unique path on this Creative Living journey.

I like to think of my creative energy as a magical superpower. When I reconnected to my creative essence in mid-life, I discovered that I was actually creating all the time, and that I could create something from almost anything, as if by magic! I came to believe that if I could transform a blank page, then I could transform my world.

When I began dabbling in creative activities again, I realized how much joy I felt when I created, and how little joy had been in my life without it. Soon, I could feel that creative energy expanding and lifting me up. Anxiety and limitation were replaced with growing curiosity and experimentation. My courage was building, too. I started to question the "rules" and wonder about new possibilities. With heightened awareness, I saw everything with new eyes. It wasn't long before I was dreaming again, and my journal is where those dreams came to life, first in written form and then in doodles and mixed media collage. And, when I got brave enough to share with other women like me, in creative play and journaling workshops, I witnessed those women shift from being afraid to make mistakes to trying crazy new things and playing with child-like abandon. Collectively, we came alive again. We experienced what it means to be present and in flow. We connected, healed and thrived in ways beyond our wildest imaginations.

What inspires me to create, you ask? I get to bear witness to these miracles manifesting through our creative imaginations and I am honored. All is well in my world.

CREATIVE TIP #76

Karen Lange is a very talented freelance writer, author and editor who embraces the idea of being creative all of the time.

Ideas are everywhere, but sometimes we don't see them at first glance. The most helpful creativity booster for me is simply observing life. From people watching to grocery shopping, you name it, there are ideas everywhere. And the good news is, these little gems can turn into bigger ideas. For example, while waiting in the checkout line at the store recently, I noticed a gentleman who reminded me of my grandfather. My imagination kicked in and I wondered, what was this man's life like when he was younger? Was he in the army? Did he own a business? What was his family like? Within seconds I had several article ideas waiting for further development.

Whether a casual writer or freelancer, I believe that cultivating observational skills helps enhance creativity. So how can we foster these ideas? By paying attention to things around us, large and small. Lay in the grass and look up at the sky. Think about things from a child's perspective. Ask questions. Daydream. Journal. Brainstorm. Make lists of words, phrases, or the blessings found in the day. Most of all, relax and have fun. We never know where our observations will take us!

CREATIVE TIP #77

Karen Rostoker Gruber is an award-winning children's book author and ventriloquist from New Jersey. Like many creative people, she doesn't limit her "creative process" to just the daylight hours.

I usually write actual stories at 3 a.m. and revise during the day. And if I'm having trouble revising a particular story during the day, I go to sleep with that issue and wake up with an answer. I write on sticky notes in the dark and fling them all over the floor at. In the morning, if I can read my 3 a.m. chicken scratch, I usually have a resolution. If you go to sleep with a question or an issue, more times than not, during REM, your brain will free up and figure it out for you.

CREATIVE TIP #78

Lee Silber's 26 book titles have sold through 94 printings and are available in five languages. Two titles were best sellers, and Lee toured bookstores in 48 states. Some of his latest books include *The Homeless Hero, Runaway Best Seller, Jimmy and the Kid* and *The Pelican*.

Creativity contrarian. I'm sure you've heard it all when it comes to creativity and the creative process. I know I have. So, I want to share some things I do that are outside the norm in the hopes that you may try them and have success, or not feel like a freak because you do something weird to get good ideas.

1. For all those people who say they sit down and write first thing in the morning (and early in the morning at that) I say sleep in and do some simple tasks to warm up. Check some things off your to-do list. Score some easy wins. Stretch your mind into shape with a few mindless warm up tasks. If you like to get your ducks in a row to start your day, I say go with what works. It's not procrastinating if you would have to do these mundane maintenance tasks later anyway.

2. In baseball the harder you try to swing or throw a ball the worse the results are. Sometimes with creativity trying too hard is also counterproductive. There are all kinds of explanations why this is, but in a nutshell, we sometimes need to occupy the critical part of brain (distract it in a way) with something unrelated to our artistic endeavor so that our creative brain can provide us with wild ideas. Taking a break may be the best thing you can do to be productive. I know, counter intuitive, but it works. (Always carry something to jot ideas down when you are out and about.

3. Let go of the outcome. Most recording artists (outside of the Beatles who once said to each other, "Let's write a swimming pool") can't just produce a hit song on demand. If they could, they would, right? With any form of art worrying about how something will be received usually impeded the creative process. Just write, paint, or create without thinking about what will happen when it's done. You can go back and polish the thing up and make it more marketable (if you want, or better yet, find someone who wants what you want to create.)

CREATIVE TIP #79

Lynn Patner is a social worker, a Transformational Life Coach and the author of *The Awakened Soul: Discovering the Light Within.*

I had a burning need to write down all my adventures of awakening to why I am here and who I am. This book was written with love so that it may assist others on their journeys. I also had a team of unseen guides who were very persistent in encouraging me to write.

Meditate and learn how to connect with your inner wisdom and ask the universe to assist you in fulfilling all your dreams. We have no idea how responsive the universe is, nor how powerful we all are.

CREATIVE TIP #80

Lisa Roberts is a Pediatric Yoga Specialist, Author and Professional Speaker.

Most of my known published works are based on my work as a pediatric yoga specialist in the clinical setting. While I certainly draw on my creativity working with children, the work flows easily when writing this material, as it's really a matter of organizing the most successful elements of my work with children and explaining how and why it is beneficial.

BUT I do love to write! Whether I have written for school or pleasure, or in my past life while helping others as a ghost writer, I have been known to compare the process of writing with childbirth: painful, grueling, and at times complicated … yet it ends with a rush of pure joy and delight along with the immense satisfaction and pride of creating something really beautiful.

CREATIVE TIP #81

Debbie Hampton is a Communications Professional, Content Creator, Writer, Online Marketer, Social Media Manager and the author of several books, including *Beat Depression and Anxiety by Changing Your Brain: With Simple Practices That Will Improve Your Life*.

How To Encourage Creativity

Like trying to squeeze water, the harder you try to be creative, the more infuriatingly impossible it often becomes. Creativity is one of those elusive things that just will not be forced...but you can learn how to encourage it.

While the right side of the brain has traditionally been credited with creative thought, recent brain scans show that creative thinking engages the whole brain through a part of the brain called the associative cortex. The associative cortex sits in the frontal, parietal, and temporal lobes of the brain linking senses, emotions, logic, social abilities, language skills, memories, movement, and thoughts in potentially novel ways.

Although you are probably not aware of it, you use your associative-creative brain every day. For instance, it allows you to recall the taste of apple pie when seeing a picture of it or recreates the thunder of a train when reading about one. Everyone has this basic level of creative thought and, while some people are naturally more imaginative than others, extraordinary creativity can be developed and encouraged.

Unlike conscious thought, creativity requires letting go, relaxing, and allowing ideas to flow without censorship, judgment, or comparison. Being creative requires an altered state of mind, different from the alert, waking state, in which logical reasoning is suspended and the mind is open to new perceptions. The more you encourage creativity, the more it flows.

Tips from neuroscientists, writers, and coaches to increase the creative juices are:

- **Get bored.** Reduce your entertainment: TV, internet, computer, video games, and movies. Boredom spurs your subconscious brain into action. Science shows that your brain's resting-state circuitry, is where it does some of its best, wisest, and most creative work.

- **Dive in.** This is the opposite of the above. Read as much as possible outside your norm. Visit art museums. Listen to new music. Get inspired. Expose your brain to novelty to spark new ideas.

- **Make it a ritual.** Build creative time into your daily routine. Whatever you're interested in, do it every day. Make encouraging creativity a habit.

- **Make a creative space.** Having a designated room, corner, or space where you have easy access to all the tools you need to be creative will help it flourish.

- **Meditate.** Meditation connects neurons more strongly, helps retrieve memories, generates new associations, reduces anxiety, and diminishes emotional blocks that can all enhance creativity.

- **Honor anxiety.** Let anxiety give you a different approach and cause you to question your habitual ways of doing things, but don't let it stop the process.

- **Make a mistake.** Quiet any perfectionist pressure by letting yourself mess up already. When I write, I like to let myself just write anything. It's easier to get something written and go back and revise than put a lot of pressure on myself to "get it right."

- **Get up and move.** The movement cortex of the brain is also involved in thinking and emotions. Movement oxygenates and activates your mind. Take a walk, exercise, have sex, stretch and then resume.

- **Let go.** Let go of old habits and embrace new perspectives. Step out of your routine. Write with your nondominant hand. Do something you've never done before. Get your brain out of its comfort zone.

- **Reframe the problem.** Assume a new vantage point – look at the issue from a different side or above or below. Ask new questions or the opinions of others. Be curious.

- **Create a "crummy" version first.** Just get started. Allow yourself to create without any judgement or critiquing.

Creativity is a vital dimension of human which can be activated through intention and attention. Instead of chasing creativity, let it catch you!

CREATIVE TIP #82

Michelle Lores is a Christian author of over 100 books. Her prayer is that the words she writes would always be in line with the absolute Truth of God's Word, the Bible, and would bring God's Light to all who read them.

Inspiration
By Michelle Lores Copyright 2022

Inspiration strikes
At the least expected times.
A picture, a phrase–
A word that stays
And sticks out in most unexpected ways.

But somehow, I know
That the thought will grow
Into something beautiful.
And so, I develop
Thought after thought
Until I have something truly meaningful.

CREATIVE TIP #83

Chrysa Smith is a talented author and no stranger to the creative world. Her books include *The Adventures of the Poodle Posse Series, Once Upon a Poodle, A Grand Slam Birthday, The*

Upside-Down Gardner and many more. Visit wellbredbook.net to learn more.

I've been a writer for a long time. I love finding an idea that might interest people and a matching niche for telling that story to the world. I've met the most interesting people, learned about a great many skills and improved my craft along the way. That's been part of my creativity—but there's more.

When the deadlines were passed and I was in writer's limbo, I found myself watching my dogs. Their dastardly antics led to me wanting to tell them—-but to kids? I had not a bit of experience here. So, I wrote a rough draft, took some children's writing classes and ventured out.

The 'Poodle Posse' series came out of it, with five books (Ages 6-9) spurred by my pet adventures, their personalities or scenarios that I wanted to see play out. From there, a prequel picture book for younger audiences, and I fizzled on pooches.

But a thwarted gardening experiment, in which I planted a root the wrong way, led to The Upside-Down Gardener—-a magical gardening story. This is followed by A Grand Slam Birthday, in which the protagonist is thrust into a different situation she must navigate her way around.

When I visit with school students, I tell them there are ideas everywhere. The creative person sees the little, brilliant gem in the everyday, and spins it into something noteworthy.

CREATIVE TIP #84

Laura Briggs is known as The Freelance Coach, and is a prolific writer, speaker and author. Her latest book is *Remote Work for Military Spouses.*

Absorb places, people, and situations whenever you can. Whether traveling in another country, taking a walk in a park you've been to hundreds of times, or simply listening to a news story, look for unique ideas and concepts. How do people respond to one another and what can you learn about them from that? What kinds of circumstances make life interesting? Whenever I am in idea-gathering mode, I read, listen, and watch everything I can.

Record it in a notebook and review that on a regular basis to see which ideas might match up together. These could turn into essays, short stories, or even novels. If something caught your attention, it might be worth noting down and seeing how you can be inspired by reality!

CREATIVE TIP #85

Peggy Sue Wells is the bestselling author of 29 books translated into eight languages including The *What To Do* series, *The Slave Across the Street, Slavery in the Land of the Free, Bonding With Your Child Through Boundaries, The Girl Who Wore Freedom, Homeless for the Holidays, Chasing Sunrise, The Marc Wayne series,* and *The Ten Best Decisions A Single Mom Can Make.*

Ways to be creative:

Get a cat and name it Muse. Then you always have the muse with you.

Write. Some days we write well, other days not so much. Just write. Put black letters on the white manuscript and polish later.

Writing is a team sport. Gather a positive team around you who wants to see you succeed, and can give feedback that moves you forward. If you feel worse after being with your critique partner(s) than before, they are not the chosen one.

Always be learning. Like being a musician, writing is a craft we perpetually practice and hone.

Always have a mentor.

Be audacious, outrageous in crafting story. Put your character in a new setting – on a dog sled, in Amish country, at the south pole, on a movie backlot, in a factory that makes plastic doggie poop.

Heighten suspense by writing from the point of view of the character who has the most to lose.

Research a weird fact and add the fact to the story. Like what's the capital of North Dakota, how often does a goose poop (every 8 minutes – trust me on this one), or what's the difference between a violin and a fiddle?

Ask what if the character goes spelunking? What if they lose what they most love, get what they most want, run for supreme court judge, get trapped in a moon launch, are despised by paparazzi, stalked by a younger sibling, allergic to peanuts, have a romantic crush on a bull rider, have one leg two inches shorter than the other, get a mysterious text, are mistaken for someone else, wrongly accused, go blind, invent a mean people warning device, get the wrong vaccination, run away from the dog, disguise themselves to spy on someone, discover their parent has a secret identity, design the White House Christmas card, make the wrong decision for all the right reasons, become the presidential kid's shopping nanny, find Santa has run away from the North Pole and joined the ice follies?

Visit new places, have fresh experiences so you have something to write about.

Recall how your most painful experience looked, smelled, tasted, sounded, felt? Write a scene that plunges your character into those strong emotions.

When editing, take out these banned words: said, really, very, just, literally, it, thing, still, even, also, oh, yeah, hello, good-bye, up, down.

CREATIVE TIP #86

Shannon Anderson is an award-winning children's book author and national speaker. She taught for 25 years, from first grade through college level, and was named one of the 10 teachers who "awed and inspired" The Today Show in 2019. Shannon loves doing author visits to schools, mentoring aspiring writers and keynoting at events.

For me, creativity starts with a well-lit, quiet, comfy space, my laptop or a notepad, and possibly one or three furry friends by my side.

If it is a new piece of work, I will generate lists on the topic, theme, or character I'm trying to showcase. This could include synonyms, phrases, quotes, rhyming words, puns, and related ideas.

I also start to look at mentor texts, images, and videos - both nonfiction and fictionalized. Once my wheels are in motion, I can begin to figure out the structure my piece will take and make my first attempts at that messy, but glorious first draft.

CREATIVE TIP #87

Valerie J. Lewis Coleman is an award-winning author of numerous books, including *Do It Right the First Time: How to Write, Publish, and Market Your Bestseller*. Learn more about her books and services at penofthewriter.com.

My clients often say, "Valerie, I can't make time to write."

My reply is always the same, "You cannot *make* time, but you can prioritize it."

How? By using a planning calendar and honoring your commitment to write. I created a weekly planning calendar with hourly blocks from 6 AM to 8 PM (I am not creative early morning or late evening) and these steps:

- Fill in the calendar with the must-dos for the week: work, school, kids' activities, church.
- Available blocks of writing time will magically appear.
- Commit to write at specific times by scheduling it; otherwise, it won't happen.
- Maintain integrity in your schedule. Set times and adhere to them, or you'll be in the same place this time next year.
- Start small - 15 minutes or 150 words per day - and then build to avoid frustration and feeling overwhelmed.

That's all for now...hope you have enjoyed and been inspired by everything in this journal.

We'll let Alan Alda, who played the role of Hawkeye Pierce on the award-winning television show, *M*A*S*H*, leave you with some words of wisdom you should always remember:

You have to leave the city of your comfort zone and go into the wilderness of your intuition. What you'll discover will be wonderful. What you discover will be yourself.

Five brothers served.
Only two came home.

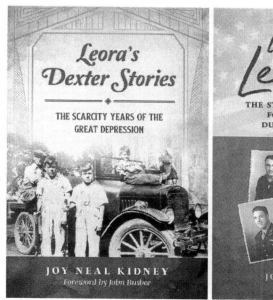

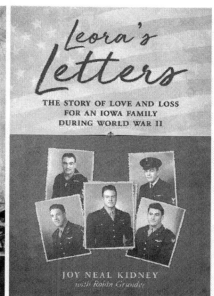

Beaverdale Books ships autographed copies.

Paperbacks and ebooks through Amazon
Leora's Letters also on Audible

---

http://joynealkidney.com
joynealkidney@gmail.com

Part journal, part devotional, part ramblings of a middle-aged woman, *Well Loved: Just As I Am* is exactly as the title implies. It's the good, the bad, and the ugly from a woman who struggles but knows that God is faithful. God offers answers to our brokenness and will make a way for us. Barb's sense of humor and vulnerability make this book unique.

If you are wondering whether God really loves you, and if you matter, then this book is for you.

Barb has written two other books, a humorous look at parenting called *All My Favorite Colors are Red* and a Bible study about 10 Old Testament characters called *All My Favorite Heroes are Dead*. You can find them on Amazon.

KEEP
CALM

READ

SCAN ME

DeanaBean.com

I Am Proud of Who I Am is a 15-book series written as a way to introduce students to different places and cultures across the world

"Put simply, this book was therapy for me. I am much more at ease with myself now, and I will always be in Debbie's debt for helping with that. Read it. My bet is that you will take away a greater understanding of yourself."

MRJT

"A life-changing read."

sexsuicideserotonin.com

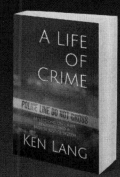

NICOLE GABOR

catwalk
a novel

Eighteen-year-old shy, suburban aspiring model Catherine Watson longed for adventure, for a life less ordinary and moves away to pursue her modeling dream in New York City. When she is "discovered" by the hottest fashion designer in the pages of Vogue magazine, "Cat" thinks she has it all as the New York fashion world's new "It" girl.

Her life is thrust into an alternate universe, where star-studded cocktail parties, casting calls, go-sees, and nightclub openings revolve around her like constellations and she tries to play the part. Her former self, "Catherine," was now a shadow of who she was, and what she was becoming. Leaving her good-girl image behind, Cat quickly learns things aren't always what they seem on the catwalk, and she's faced with a decision that will change her life forever.

Drawing on her own experiences as a model in the fast-paced fashion industry, author Nicole Gabor masterfully weaves a timeless story of self-discovery, coming of age, and the perils of first loves.

Made in the USA
Columbia, SC
25 January 2025

52557034R00070